MW00440378

Be Exceptional!

Jenny

TESTIMONIALS

"The Exceptional Leaders Playbook is very insightful as to human nature, leadership and the relationships within an organization."

Joe Robson, President & Founder, The Robson Companies

"Leadership is a skill that requires constant study and attention. This book is for any leader that is serious about developing high performing teams. Having worked with Tracy Spears and Wally Schmader for a number of years I can attest that they are relatable and provide strategies that are immediately executable".

Steve Richards, President & CEO, Mood Media

"Exceptional Leaders Playbook provides a fresh perspective and a clear, articulate guide for leaders looking to strengthen their ability to lead their people and organizations to success!"

Anna Goldenberg, CEO, True Impact Coaching

"Whatever your current role in business, education, non-profit or community, Spears and Schmader highlight the important attributes that are core to effective leadership in an engaging and self-reflective format."

Dennis Neill, Program Officer,
Charles & Lynn Schusterman Family Foundation

"Wally Schmader & Tracy Spears lay out a readable and detailed plan that anyone can use to become a much better leader."

Chris Bene, Managing Director, Brock Capital

"Have you ever considered the cost of mediocrity? This playbook is an investment in your success as a leader."

Deb Wiggs, Founder/Tranformationist,
V2V Management Solutions

"For anyone who has doubts that leadership skills are learnable, the Exceptional Leaders Playbook is a must-read. It is an insightful practical guide for any leader, no matter your experience level, who is committed to improving their leadership skills."

Jim Bender, Attorney, Hall Lentil Law Firm

"I picked this book up and I didn't want to put it down. I wanted to continue reading to find out how to differentiate myself from the average leader. I don't want to be average any longer. How do I start to differentiate myself from other leaders? I'm going to start by reading this book."

Lora Zumwalt, QuikTrip Vice President Accounting-Controller

"The issues discussed in this book are issues that all leaders struggle with, and the practical suggestions put forth are surprisingly easy to implement. Another engaging and powerful leadership book from Tracy Spears and Wally Schmader!"

Annie Tomecek, Global Community Relations,
T.D. Williamson, Inc.

"In Tracy Spears & Wally Schmader's *Exceptional Leaders Playbook,* corporate leaders receive a smart, strategic, simple, play-by-play coaching blueprint designed to get rid of the negatives and fast-track the positives."

Pamela McKissick Former Co-Owner & CEO
at Williams &Williams

EXCEPTIONAL LEADERS PLAYBOOK

HIGH-IMPACT COACHING STRATEGIES FOR TODAY'S PROGRESSIVE LEADERS

TRACY SPEARS

&

WALLY SCHMADER

Published by Motivational Press, Inc.
1777 Aurora Road
Melbourne, Florida, 32935
www.MotivationalPress.com

Copyright 2018 © by Tracy Spears & Wally Schmader

All Rights Reserved

No part of this book may be reproduced or transmitted in any form by any means: graphic, electronic, or mechanical, including photocopying, recording, taping or by any information storage or retrieval system without permission, in writing, from the authors, except for the inclusion of brief quotations in a review, article, book, or academic paper. The authors and publisher of this book and the associated materials have used their best efforts in preparing this material. The authors and publisher make no representations or warranties with respect to accuracy, applicability, fitness or completeness of the contents of this material. They disclaim any warranties expressed or implied, merchantability, or fitness for any particular purpose. The authors and publisher shall in no event be held liable for any loss or other damages, including but not limited to special, incidental, consequential, or other damages. If you have any questions or concerns, the advice of a competent professional should be sought.

Manufactured in the United States of America.

ISBN: 978-1-62865-498-1

CONTENTS

FOREWORD

WELCOME TO THE Exceptional Leaders Playbook! The fact that you are interested in this title means one thing… you are looking for actionable strategies to be a better leader and coach.

We are proud to say our most recent book, "What Exceptional Leaders Know" achieved best seller status and opened many doors that allowed our company, The Exceptional Leaders Lab, to work with some amazing clients. Some of those clients include: Wal-Mart, Coca-Cola, PWC Price-Waterhouse-Coopers, Maersk, OneGas, Fast Company, Cargill, TE Connectivity, Medical Group Managers Association, WPX Energy, TSI, QuikTrip, Video Gaming Technologies, and dozens more.

The most exciting thing about the response to W.E.L.K. was the immediate feedback we received after publishing the book. We heard from dozens of leaders, and the feedback came from people all over the leadership spectrum; C-suite executives, middle managers, brand new leaders, coaches, sales managers; leaders of all kinds. Most of the feedback was very specific and focused on two areas:

1. Our readers really appreciated the practical and actionable content. Not leadership philosophy, not leadership theory and not academic leadership studies; but real world-tested recommendations and tactics. Strategies they could put into play immediately, and they wanted more.

2. They appreciated the parts of W.E.L.K. that were focused on how leaders can improve themselves and how they can get better at the craft of leadership. They understood that exceptional leadership starts with an exceptional skill set.

Here are a few of the comments we received:

» "It is very hard to find real tactics, I mean actual "to-do's", in leadership books. I was able to start leveraging a few of your recommendations immediately."

» "It seems like most of the management content I see is basically focused on how to manipulate people into doing things they don't want to do. It is refreshing to see a different approach."

» "Let's face it, many of today's leaders and managers don't know how to connect with the younger people coming into their organization. They think they need to try to change them somehow, when the truth is that it is the leaders themselves who need to evolve and improve."

» "Why do the leadership books and seminars leave out the specifics? I mean things like; what do you actually say to people to help them improve and do a better job? And, how do you actually create transparency? I have an MBA from a reputable college and I never had one class dedicated to influencing people to get better. I appreciated the practical approach of What Exceptional Leaders Know."

» "My least favorite thing about leadership coaches is how heavily they lean on the motivational aspect of leadership. You really don't find this in any other profession. Only in management (and especially sales management) do we believe that motivating people is part of our job. Your book focused on real tactics, not the short-term motivational tactics found in most management books".

» "Many of the executives in our organization don't really know how to be a progressive leader. They are basically doing everything the same way they did 10 or 15 years ago. I am concerned that they are working themselves out of jobs. I would love to have some more leadership-specific coaching for them."

There were more, but those statements give you the feel for a lot of the feedback from the book. We paid close attention to those two strongest themes to our feedback, and determined that we could deliver even more of what our readers want in a second book. Further, we were very excited to discover that there was an enthusiastic audience for a "leadership book" with such a strong self-development emphasis.

We decided that the Exceptional Leaders Playbook could be structured in such a way that would allow us to deliver more of what we know the most progressive leaders in the world are doing to drive extraordinary results, along with specific and proven ways for leaders to drastically improve their personal skill sets.

At the end of each chapter we'll give you some space to capture your thoughts and potential action items. The headings will be "The One Thing" where we encourage you to capture the most important take-away from the chapter, and "Playbook Notes" where we hope you will record tactics and actions you intend to take. Every once in a while, you will come across a picture of a whistle. This means that what follows is an actionable coaching point we are recommending.

You're going to find a lot of recommended exercises and self-analysis in this book. We encourage you to experience this book as a participant, and not just a reader. Dig in, test our strategies: we want to be a partner in your leadership development.

INTRODUCTION

ANYONE WHO STUDIES organizational performance knows that leadership is the pivot-point between low- and high-performing teams. It doesn't matter what your organization or business does. It doesn't matter how long your team has been doing what they do, it doesn't matter where you are: Leadership is the difference between success and failure for any organization over the long term.

When we talk about leadership in this book, we will be talking about leadership as a verb, not leadership as a noun. As far as we're concerned, leadership is something that you do, leadership is pure influence... and coaching is leadership in action.

AVERAGE LEADERSHIP = AVERAGE RESULTS

A few years ago, we met a consultant who had worked with several national retailers. His specialty was improving the customer experience to increase customer loyalty. One of his clients was one of the large national office supply chains. They had asked him to collect some data on how customers felt about their brand. Specifically, they wanted to understand the shopping experience from the customer's point of view... and the overall brand impression those customer had after visiting one of their stores. They were in a very competitive retail segment, office supplies, and wanted to know if their brand was differentiated in their customer's eyes.

His researchers were posted outside dozens of his client's stores in locations all over the country. His team also gathered the same information from two national competitor's stores also in different locations in the U.S. The researchers' job was simple: They would interview customers as they left the office supply stores. The first question was the simplest: "Which store did you just leave?". Often the customers were holding a bag or walking underneath a big sign with the store's name on it.

Shockingly, just half of the respondents got it right. Only around 50% of the customers could name the office supply store they had just walked into and out of. The wrong answers were always the two other competitive stores. Why? These competitive businesses were all so similar as to be indistinguishable from each other: The stores were the same sizes, they were laid out similarly, they sold the same products, and their advertising, promotions and prices were comparable. The only meaningful differentiator between these national competitors was the locations of their stores. Customers had no brand loyalty at all... they were just going to the closest one.

Why are we citing this research? Because so many would-be leaders have positioned themselves in the same way. They've not differentiated themselves from other leaders and coaches. Our experience shows that the skill-sets of leaders at different levels are amazingly similar. Front line leaders and managers, mid-level leaders and coaches, and executive and C-suite leaders all have surprisingly similar approaches to their jobs. If you remove the different industries and cultures, many of these leaders would be interchangeable.

They use the same lingo and clichés, use the same programs and technical tools, have the same influences, are focused on the same issues, and are motivated by the same things. We are not trying to marginalize leaders, we're just constantly surprised by how willing leaders are tomarginalize themselves. Just like the office supply stores, most leaders do not differentiate themselves enough to change the expectations or outcomes people have when working with them. They have allowed themselves to be generic.

THERMOSTATS & THERMOMETERS

The difference between effective and ineffective leadership is the difference between a thermostat and a thermometer. The thermometer will tell you the temperature. It can accurately measure what is happening in the environment.

Most managers are thermometers. The thermostat sets the temperature. It dictates what the environment is going to be. It can make people comfortable or uncomfortable. It can change things quickly when necessary. It's simple: exceptional leaders are thermostats, not thermometers.

Here are some examples of thermometer and thermostat leadership actions, you will see the difference immediately.

Thermometer – Measuring, reviewing, reporting, analyzing, revising

Thermostat – Training, engaging, inspiring, coaching, expecting

Progressive leaders are active and deliberate influencers. They influence direction, priorities, morale, expectations, goals, and culture. Most importantly, they influence people. Here is where the leader-as-coach takes center stage. Every coach knows exactly what their job is, it's in their title.

A coach knows that they are successful to the degree that they can influence the people they're working with. Not all leaders understand this simple idea. A leader never has to wonder whether they are succeeding in their role or not, the evidence is right in front of them every day of the week. Is the team gradually improving? Do the organizational results reflect this improvement? Are their people passionate about their jobs? If the answer to those two questions is yes, the leader is succeeding. If the answer is no, then the leader is not positively influencing people and outcomes.

Here's where things get interesting. Because leadership is a craft and not an art, it can be learned. Leaders who aspire to be high-impact influencers can learn to coach effectively and change their teams and organizations for the better. There are reliable tactics and techniques that form the foundation of exceptional leadership. They are absolutely learnable and can be implemented almost immediately by any progressive leader.

This is what the "Exceptional Leaders Playbook" is all about. In the pages of this book we will be focusing on actionable tactics and techniques that will allow you to add to your leadership skill-set immediately. The sections in the book are designed to be read in any order you prefer, and jumping around between topics is encouraged.

We'll begin the "Exceptional Leaders Playbook" with a segment focused on some of the most reliable high-impact tactics leaders can leverage to improve themselves. We will look inward first, with the intent of then facing outward as much more capable and dynamic leaders.

Are you ready? Let's get started.

EVERYTHING STARTS WITH THE COACH

> "What good is an idea if it remains an idea? Try. Experiment. Fail. Try again. Change the world."
>
> **-Simon Sinek**

LEADERSHIP IS A VERB

It's TIME FOR US ALL TO stop thinking about leadership as a position, an aspiration or a reward. You can never "arrive" at leadership, and no one else can make you a leader. Leadership is a verb. Leadership is something you do.

This pivot in thinking is incredibly important for progressive leaders. Being able to distinguish "verb leadership" from "noun leadership" is crucial for anybody who really wants to make a meaningful difference working with other people.

Here are the five reasons why:

1. **Verb leadership is all about influence**. Leaders make a positive difference on other people. It is as simple as that. Leadership is visible and quantifiable. You can easily see when it's there... and you can see when it's not.

2. **Verb leadership is inclusive**. Anybody who can influence positive action towards a worthy goal or objective is a leader. By this definition everyone is empowered to leadership and

it has nothing to do with what is on their business card or where they fit in the org chart.

3. **Verb leadership doesn't wait**. In traditional thinking, someone else has to make you a leader. You need a promotion or a specific title. You might need some seniority or a certain amount of experience in your role. The truth is that effective leadership is all about intelligent and positive action. It doesn't need permission… it only needs intention.

4. **Verb leadership takes courage**. The ability to act is what makes a leader valuable. We all know that results don't come from opinions… results come from actions. Who on your team is actually starting things? Who are your initiators? Consensus, analysis and commentary do not move the needle.

5. **Verb leadership drives accountability**. Great leaders are defined by what they do, not what they know. Progressive organizations know how to recognize and reward action-oriented leaders.

Final thought: <u>Leadership leaves clues</u>. Your team is a clear and accurate reflection of your leadership. Are people getting better over time? Is there more capability in your organization or department? Are expectations rising? Is there tangible momentum toward a better future? These are the irrefutable evidence of leadership.

Leadership is influence. Leadership is something you do. It is behavior. Leadership is a verb.

The One Thing: _____

_____

Playbook Notes: _____

_____

_____

_____

_____

> "Leadership is a potent combination of strategy and character, but if you must be without one… be without a strategy."
> **-Norman Schwarzkopf**

TOXIC BELIEFS FOR LEADERS

WE HAVE STUDIED MANY organizations over the years, and it's clear that most of them excel to whatever degree their leaders believe in the talent, possibilities, and potential of their people. That sounds like a hopeful platitude that you might find on a motivational poster somewhere, doesn't it? Apply this premise to situations you have worked in, and the leaders you have worked with: Organizations excel to whatever degree their leaders believe in the talent, possibilities, and potential of their people. I'm sure you'll agree that it's true.

Think about some of the businesses that you are most familiar with. You can probably think of businesses and organizations across the whole range from total believers in their people to very cynical companies who believe they can succeed despite the shortcomings of their people.

You can see reflections of how a company feels about its people every direction you look. Organizations that allow and promote a diversity of opinion, accept mannerly disputes, acknowledge excellence wherever it's found, and share information liberally, generally have a higher level of person-for-person productivity than more bureaucratic organizations. The worst offenders of this theory are companies in which upper management consistently underestimates their own people's talent and capabilities.

We've had an opportunity to work with many different organizations, representing several different industries, and it's been surprising to see how pervasive some of this thinking is. Here is where sales organizations are generally more progressive. They know they absolutely depend on the performance and capability or their people.

There are lots of quantitative measures available that will show comparative per-person revenue in organizations. You can imagine the disparity between the firms where people are allowed and expected to grow in responsibility while being challenged to improve and those organizations where people are kept in categories and classifications, pre-determined by management. What's really surprising is that the organizations that are most in need of new talent and new ideas are often the ones who are most guilty of "pigeon-holing" their own people.

Another shocking and dangerous problem we see again and again is in organizations that believe their organizational chart is also their intelligence and talent chart. That is to say, they really believe that the distribution of titles in their business is an accurate reflection of talent, intellect, and creativity. It's easy to see how many issues this idea would cause; suppression of new talent, ego-centricity in management, under-recognition of grass roots ideas, etc.

We refer to these kinds of growth-crushing ideas as "toxic beliefs." These are concepts, thought patterns and ideas that, when adopted and absorbed at the leadership level, can wound or even kill an organization from the inside out.

Below are some toxic beliefs that exist in many organizations today. These reflect the leader's personal beliefs that have been slowly absorbed into the organization. Many of these beliefs are toxic enough to gradually kill a business. You will recognize some of them.

- » People will do as little work as they possibly can.
- » The status quo represents the least risk for our organization.
- » Good ideas start at the top.
- » We can cost-cut our way to growth.
- » We must keep people feeling like their jobs are at risk.
- » The numbers are telling the whole story.
- » Leadership is a "soft skill".
- » Full disclosure is not an option.
- » Our people value security over recognition.
- » Tenure = ability.
- » People are what they are.
- » Our managers know how to lead effectively.
- » Diversity applies only to race and gender.
- » We don't need to invest in leadership development
- » Our organizational chart mirrors our intellectual level.
- » Our executives don't need to work on their skill sets.
- » It is easier to hire productivity than it is to develop it ourselves.

» We talk like a democracy, but act like a dictatorship.

Amazingly, this is the short list. Do you recognize any of them? It's easy for any progressive leader to see how just one or two of these beliefs, when held by a number of powerful people, could actually destroy the culture of an organization.

Where do these kinds of toxic beliefs come from? They are usually formed as a bias in the would-be leader. They take root there, and when the idea goes unchallenged for a period of time, it becomes a "truth" in the mind of that leader. Decisions are made based on the toxic belief and it becomes "socialized" in the organization. It's just a given that this belief is true.

Sometimes, someone new will come into an organization and identify a toxic belief immediately. This is an important part of a management consultant's job. Often the toxic belief is so entrenched that even after it is identified and disproven, it can't be removed. This is actually the root cause of most executive reassignments. A toxic belief, or set of beliefs, can only be eliminated or stopped by removing the leader responsible for them.

The bottom line here is that we need to be careful about which thoughts we allow to stay in our heads. If they are limiting beliefs, and if they cause us to question the capabilities of our people, they may be toxic to the growth and success of our organizations.

The One Thing: _____

_____

Playbook Notes: _____

_____

_____

_____

_____

> "We all have a blind spot and it's shaped exactly like us"
>
> **-Junot Diaz**

LEADERSHIP BLIND SPOTS

L EADERSHIP BLIND SPOTS are the specific areas where a leader, even a very successful leader, is missing something. A blind spot can be a lack of attention to a certain area, or a part of your skill set that never really developed.

All leaders have blind spots. Why is this? Because success in certain leadership areas can obscure needed development in other areas. It's a form of compensation. Our strengths in some areas can be leveraged to partially, but never completely, offset a weakness.

When a progressive leader discovers a blind spot, they have also discovered upside opportunity for themselves. It doesn't matter whether you discover them yourself or if someone else points out a blindspot for you, it's always a positive thing when you can acknowledge a blind spot.

It's important to always remember that leadership is a verb. It is something you do. As leaders we want to eliminate blindspots that will keep us from effectively leading our teams. Let's discuss the three most common blindspots we see in leaders:

FORGETTING ABOUT THE "WHY"

Sometimes leaders and managers get so caught up with targets and tactics that they can forget why their people are even coming to work. They knew it when they started in management, but over time even good leaders gradually forget that their goals, or the companies goals, are not the same their people's goals.

Fact: every single person on your team has their own unique reasons for coming to work. This is their "Why". Many leaders are completely out of touch with this truth. Some have never even considered it. This can be a high blind spot for a leader. If you are serious about driving high performance through your organization, you will need to the hard work of getting in touch with everyone's "Why".

NOT GRASPING THE IMPORTANCE OF STRAIGHT TALK

As leaders move up the ranks, they tend to be more data-driven, spending most of their time in meetings with people other than those they are leading. Here's what happens next: they begin to spend more time talking about their people than they do talking to their people. This blind spot will often appear when a leader has moved way up the org chart. Some leaders will even begin to actively avoid uncomfortable conversations with the people they are responsible to.

People deserve straight talk from their leaders. Clear, direct and understandable communication should be your objective, especially when the topic is sensitive or when it directly affects the person you are talking to. Avoid business rhetoric and management buzzwords. You should use the exact same level of candor and transparency that you would appreciate from one of your superiors. Your leadership authenticity and influence will benefit from this kind of no fluff, no BS communication.

NOT UNDERSTANDING THE DISTINCTION BETWEEN CAN'T & WON'T

This may be the most important distinction you will ever learn as a leader. Leaders and managers who never learn to discern between **Can't** and **Won't** situations will have a career of frustration and confusion. In our workshops, we go so far as to say that if this distinction is all you know as a manager, you will still be more effective in your role than 50% of all leaders. Understanding the seemingly simple distinction between the two is the key to making good personnel decisions as a leader. Here are the simple definitions:

Can't – They just don't know how to do it. It's a capability issue.

Won't – They refuse to do it, either passively or actively.

It's a motivational issue.

Leaders can create serious issues for themselves when they misdiagnose a situation and treat a Can't like a Won't… or vice versa. It prevents them from coaching and managing people successfully. It's a blind spot that some leaders carry through their whole careers.

Figuring out exactly where a performance issue is rooted is crucial to successful leadership. When you start with an accurate assessment of whether a personnel issue is a Can't or a Won't, you are going to make the right decision about how to respond to the situation. We'll discuss this process in much more detail later. For now let's just agree that it is Leadership 101: Look at the roots, not the fruit.

So those are the three leadership blind spots we see most often in experienced leaders and managers. Think about your own leadership and see if any of them apply to you. Here's some good news: once a leader is able to identify a blind spot, they are well on their way to correcting it. The biggest challenge is just being able to see and acknowledging the blind spot.

Final word: blind spots keep a leader from having the leverage and influence they should. Be sensitive to them, work on them, and you can put them in in the rearview mirror where they belong.

The One Thing: _____

_____

Playbook Notes: _____

_____

_____

_____

_____

> "No matter how smart they are, most people usually only see what they're already looking for, and that's all."
> **-Veronica Roth**

UNCONSCIOUS BIAS & LEADERSHIP

U NCONSCIOUS BIAS, and the effect it has on teams and organizations, is one of the most serious leadership challenges today. There are lots of reason for this, but let's start with the most obvious one: Any business risk that is not conscious or immediately understood is daunting. Let's start by getting on the same page with a definition:

Unconscious biases are social stereotypes about certain groups of people that individuals form outside of their own conscious awareness. Everyone holds unconscious beliefs about various social and identity groups, and these biases stem from one's tendency to organize social worlds by categorizing people.

The organizational risks that come with unconscious biases are serious. Almost everything can be affected; hiring, meetings, teamwork, performance reviews, innovation, promotions, consensus-building and much more. The easiest was to see unconscious bias is to look for its effects and outcomes.

Often a team or organization will deny any kind of unconscious biases when the effects of those biases are right in front of them. In a recent project we were discussing the issue with a client who flatly denied the existence of biases in their business. This organization had the narrowest range of diversity and experience we had ever seen; the six members of the executive team were between the ages of 48-55, all male, all heterosexual, and all white.

With a small group like this you can only expect a certain amount of diversity, but it would still be almost impossible to form a group like this over time without unconscious bias driving some decisions. There is clearly something other than individual performance being recognized in this organization, and there are a LOT of organizations just like this. Most of these teams and businesses are not being overt or malicious in any way. Some are actually very progressive and still end up being carbon copies. This is unconscious bias at work.

UNCONSCIOUS BIAS AFFECTS TEAM PERFORMANCE & PROFITABILITY

Exceptional leaders have lots of admirable and important reasons to work on limiting the effect of unconscious bias in their organizations. One of the best reasons is performance. Studies have shown again and again that diverse companies perform better. One of the most concise and compelling reports was produced by the CEB Corporate Leadership Council. It was their Global Labor Market Survey, and the results were conclusive.

When employees view their workplaces as diverse and inclusive, the organizations profits exceed their non-diverse competitors. Here are the numbers:

1.12x More Discretionary Effort

1.19x Greater Intent to Stay with Organization

1.57x More Collaboration Among Teams

1.42x Greater Team Commitment

The bottom line in this report, and many others like it, is that diversity is a performance accelerant. Unconscious bias is diversity's most powerful enemy.

Let's review the five unconscious biases that directly impact the workplace:

AFFINITY BIAS

Tendency to warm up to people like ourselves

HALO EFFECT

Tendency to think everything about a person is good because you like them

PERCEPTION BIAS

Tendency to form stereotypes and assumptions about certain groups

CONFIRMATION BIAS

Tendency for people to seek information that confirms pre-existing beliefs

GROUPTHINK

Occurs when people try too hard to fit into a particular group by mimicking others or holding back thoughts and opinions

In our experience, once a certain kind of unconscious bias has a name it's a lot easier to address.

Every form of unconsious bias creates risk for a team. Progressive leaders need to understand these risks. Take a moment to think through the risks and negative outcomes that could be assoctaed with each kind of unconscious bias in your workplace:

Affinity Bias: _____

Halo Effect: _____

Perception Bias: _____

Confirmation Bias: _____

GroupThink: _____

WHERE DOES UNCONSCIOUS BIAS COME FROM?

The root of unconscious bias is our survival instinct. Our brains evolved to help us survive. Our ability to subconsciously process thousands of pieces of information in an instant kept our ancestors from becoming food.

This same ability now gets us through the day without having to slowly process every decision we need to make. The numbers from the experts make this very clear: We all receive 11 million bits of information every moment and we're only able to process about 40 bits. So our conscious mind is processing only a minute fraction of what our unconscious mind is processing. So, our unconscious mind is making

99.999996% of all of our decisions. That's a lot.

Everyone has biases; its part of being human. It's important to not be ashamed of this basic fact. Part of developing your leadership to respond to unconscious bias is accepting this truth: You are biased. So are we. And it matters.

WORKPLACE TRIGGERS FOR UNCONSCIOUS BIAS

Identifying the situations where unconscious bias happens is a crucial key for leaders. Here are the four most common triggers:

Assigning Tasks: We assign certain jobs to certain kinds of people.

Groups & Lists: When looking at a group, we use biases to analyze people and the outlying demographics tend to suffer.

Lack of Clarity: When information is lacking, our brains fill the gaps with what we think we know.

State of the Perceiver: Any heightened emotional state can keep the conscious mind distracted and disengaged.

In our experience, people tend to understand and agree that these situations are real and can trigger unconscious biases. Having conversations about these situations is a huge step in limiting the ongoing bias in your organization.

GOOGLE'S FOUR-POINT PLAN TO FIGHT UNCONSCIOUS BIAS

Google (now Alphabet) has been one of the most progressive corporations in bringing attention to institutional biases, and what companies can do to fight them. They have had an intensive ongoing organizational plan to fight unconscious bias, and it is working. Google has reported very positive and encouraging results from their efforts.

Here's a summary that will help any leader understand the formal steps necessary to reduce the unconscious bias in their business, department or organization.

STEP ONE – STRUCTURE FOR SUCCESS

» Set concrete criteria for certain jobs

» Have structured & scripted job interviews

STEP TWO – MEASURE RESULTS

» You can't improve what you can't measure

» Removing biases will change things is visible ways

» Know exactly what you are trying to change

STEP THREE – EVALUATE SUBTLE MESSAGES

» Recognize the power in signals

» Unconscious bias can hide in plain sight

» Make it someone's job to find it

STEP FOUR – HOLD EVERYONE ACCOUNTABLE

» Coach your people to question first impressions

» Everyone needs to justify decisions

» Create a culture of calling out unconscious bias

Google's four steps are not easy. Beginning to reverse something as intractable as unconscious bias is a serious undertaking, but the payoff can be huge.

This is an area where a leader and coach can really excel, and it all starts with a decision. Exceptional leaders talk about unconscious bias openly, they model and prioritize progressive approaches to the problem. Make it a priority.

The One Thing: _____

_____

Playbook Notes: _____

_____

_____

_____

_____

> "The bottom line is that bad managers are bad for business…
> and they're even worse for their employees."
> **-Leah Arnold-Smeets**

PEOPLE QUIT BOSSES, NOT COMPANIES

ALL OF US HAVE HEARD this statement at some point, and it turns out to be true. A recent Gallup survey showed that just over 50% of employees who have quit their job have done so to get away from their bosses. Another study, concluded in 2016, put the number right at 75%. That's a lot.

Still more research shows that the people who quit jobs are often the most valuable employees. They are people who feel like they deserve a certain kind of treatment and engagement at work… people who feel like they have better options.

HERE ARE THE TOP FIVE REASONS PEOPLE QUIT JOBS:

1. They don't want to work with their Boss
2. They want more opportunity for advancement

3. They want a better work/life balance

4. They want to earn more money

5. They were unsatisfied with the work environment

Look closely at this list. You could argue that four of the top five are actually just different ways of saying they need better leadership... and compensation wasn't even in the top three!

Progressive leaders know that you can't buy employee engagement or loyalty, they have to be earned. Retaining talented people comes down to leadership. The impact of great managers and leaders on retention and development surpasses any other job attribute.

LET'S REVIEW THE PRIMARY WAYS THAT POOR LEADERS CAN REPEL GREAT PEOPLE:

They Lack Humility - Making them unapproachable and less likely to recognize the excellent performance of others.

They Fail to Engage People's Creative Sides - Making people feel less inspired and underutilized.

They Fail to Develop People's Skills - Underestimating people's ability and potential.

They Hire and Promote the Wrong People - Favoring people who are more like them, instead of people more likely to excel.

The Undervalue Diversity and Inclusion - Failing to harness the power the collective and the value of differences.

They Fail to Share a Compelling Vision - Robbing people of enthusiasm and purpose for their work.

Think about this list, especially if you are a manager of people.

If you want fewer great people to quit you in the future... it may be time to make some adjustments to your leadership approach.

The One Thing: _____

_____

Playbook Notes: _____

_____

_____

_____

_____

> "Humility is not thinking less of yourself;
> it is thinking of yourself less."
>
> **-C.S. Lewis**

THE SURPRISING POWER OF LEADERSHIP HUMILITY

I F YOU READ "What Exceptional Leaders Know" you know how much we emphasize the importance of humility in leadership. It may be the section of that book where we received the most positive feedback from readera. Based on that feedback, we decided to expand on the topic here. Let's start with a simple definition we can work with. C.S. Lewis absolutely captured the essence of humility in the quote above. It is accurate and impactful enough that it's not necessary to add anything to it, but let's take a deeper dive into what makes humility such a crucial character trait for today's leaders.

For some reason, humility is never listed as one the top of character traits of very high-performing leaders. Some thought leaders understood its importance, people like Jim Rohn and Jim Collins, but for the most part it is overlooked. It may be because it is wrongly associated with weakness, or it may be because people don't believe that it can be learned. Whatever the reason, it would behoove any leader to make a study of humility, what it really is, and how to develop it.

Humility must be a central character trait for progressive leaders for five important reasons:

1. Humility gives you <u>upside</u> as a leader
2. It makes you <u>approachable</u>
3. Your team will <u>want</u> you to succeed
4. You will be naturally <u>empathetic</u>
5. It is what allows you to <u>influence</u> others

Many people think that humility is one of those things that people either do have or don't have. The truth is that it comes much easier for some people than others. There are managers and leaders whose lack of humility seems almost pathological, and others who are naturally humble, but could learn a lot about how to express their natural humility.

It is important to know that leadership itself can be a threat to your natural humility. Most of us actually found our way into leadership positions because of our egos Many leaders actually come to believe that they are somehow better than the people that report to them. This unspoken leadership superiority conceit has been responsible for much of the distance that exists between leaders and their people. This "authority gap" is unnecessary, and it presents a real risk to any organization. It can block the flow of trust and ideas between the leader and the people on the team who will be responsible for getting the important work done.

Another problem with leaders who lacking in humility is that they can become threatened by very developed, talented or uniquely skilled people. They react to these kinds of people as rivals, rather than assets. Think about that: A lack of humility can actually block our ability to embrace or engage talented people. What a risky liability that can be!

To earn the kind of trust and belief you will require to drive peak performance with your team, you will need to develop an individual kind of leadership humility. It is one of the non-negotiable underpinnings of exceptional leadership.

So how do you get there? How do you develop the kind of humility that demonstrates to your team that you really understand your role and respect and value theirs? We strongly recommend four books that will absolutely educate any leader on the importance and impact of humility in leaders. Here they are:

Servant Leadership - Robert Greenleaf's important book first published in 1970

Leadership is an Art – Max Depree's brief and powerful manifesto on soft skills

Love and Profit - James Autry's underappreciated and highly original book

Good to Great – Jim Collins' blockbuster welcomes humility back as a priority

What you will learn from any of these books is not about being a good person or having a moral responsibility as a leader. Those are nice things, and they can make us feel good about ourselves, but being a humble leader is more than that. It is also the path to top performance capability as a leader.

Leaders who can understand and embrace humility just outperform leaders who don't get it. Don't let the misunderstood word mislead you... embracing humility as a leader is the best approach to running an exceptional team, department or organization.

We have spent a lot of time with leaders who need to develop and to learn how to express humility as a way to improve their leadership. This experience has taught us that genuine expressive humility absolutely can be learned, and it will definitely make you a much more effective leader.

Here are the four proven ways to grow your leadership humility:

BE A CONSTANT LEARNER

- » Being in touch with all you don't know makes anyone humble
- » It is almost impossible to sound arrogant when you are in "learning mode"
- » You are a "work in progress" as a person and a leader

BE GRATEFUL

- » Staying close to the people and things you are most thankful for has a massive impact on a leader's humility
- » We all have lots to be grateful for in our lives. Keeping an

active awareness of these things opens us up to the world and will help to keep us warm and approachable

GET OUT OF THE FIRST-PERSON PRONOUN BUSINESS

There is no more accurate marker of a leader lacking humility than the habit of constantly referring to themselves in conversation. We've all met these kinds of leaders and their lack of self-awareness can be shocking. This one is easy to fix, just stop using the words "I", "Me" and "My" so much. Replace them with "We", "Us" and "Our".

Those words don't take any more time, and they fit into sentences in the same exact places as "I", "me" and "my". As progressive leaders we want to speak a collective language that gathers people in and makes them part of what is happening.

GIVE AWAY CREDIT

All of these recommendations have two things in common, they are easy to do, and most leaders don't do them. Giving away credit is just good leadership. Here are the three keys to keep in mind:

» Be self-effacing; compliments you give yourself don't count anyway

» Look for ways to make the people on your team shine, even if some of the work was yours

» Be worried about how other people look, not how you look

Those are four of the best ways to develop authentic and visible humility. You can expect to hear a lot more about the power of humility as a leadership trait in the coming months. The evidence has been piling up that it will be the most consistent attribute of truly transformative leaders and, most importantly, that it can be learned. Be progressive and embrace the character trait of humility, it will make you a better leader.

The One Thing: _____

_____

Playbook Notes: _____

_____

_____

_____

_____

> "Your brand is what people say about you
> when you are not in the room."
> **-Jeff Bezos**

YOUR REPUTATION IS YOUR BRAND

W<small>E ARE HEARING</small> a lot of talk about "personal branding" these days. It has become a trendy topic in books, blogs and seminars. Some leaders are turned off by the idea of personal branding. They think that it feels artificial or that a personal brand might be something that does not represent the best aspects of their character. Because we know that some of us are a little cynical about the idea, let's start with a definition we can agree on: **your brand is your reputation**.

Your personal brand is the sum total of your reputation at work, at home, with your friends, with people who don't know you well, and with people who do. Even though they are essentially the same thing, I like to use the word brand because it feels like a more dynamic word. Reputations seem like something that happens to you. Brands are something to be developed and improved.

Let's review ten important truths about your personal brand, please consider them carefully;

1. Your personal brand is what you are known for. It creates and perpetuates expectations about you.

2. Your brand arrives before you do, and stays after you leave.

3. It takes a lot of work to build an exceptionally positive personal brand, and very little to break it down or devalue it.

4. Personal brands can be helped or hurt by association.

5. Brands can be incredibly strong and surprisingly fragile.

6. What you think of yourself has very little to do with your personal brand.

7. There is no such thing as a neutral personal brand.

8. Your personal brand begins to build immediately with each new person you meet.

9. Your personal brand can be strongly influenced over time.

10. You are in control of your personal brand, just as you are in control of your reputation.

These ten truths about personal brands make a great primer for understanding exactly what they are, and how important your brand will be over the course of a career. For leaders, the importance of every aspect of personal branding is enhanced. The reason for this is that leaders are in the influence business, and your personal brand is at the base of your ability to influence people, outcomes, decisions and direction.

We have all worked with leaders who had little or no ability to influence outcomes or drive consensus. In most cases, this will be a leader whose job title would indicate that he or she was an influencer. This brings us to our last truth about personal brands:

11. Your personal brand is more important than your job title

It's hard to believe, but it's true. Every organization has examples of people whose influence is out of proportion with their actual jobs or titles. And it goes both ways: Big titles with little actual influence and little titles with tons of influence. That's the power of your personal brand.

Reputation and personal branding are serious issues for leaders. Every aspect of our ability to get things done with our teams depends on our ability to successfully influence behavior, decisions and eventual outcomes. Leaders can't afford to let their personal brand develop accidentally. It needs to be considered, reviewed and curated.

GENERIC LEADERSHIP

Career momentum has a negative affect on most leaders personal brands. Left unchecked, most leaders will end up with a very "vanilla" brand or reputation. It certainly won't be associated with strength, thought leadership, innovation or influence. It probably would not be what you would want for yourself.

Most leaders and managers are saying the same things, offering up the same leadership cliché's, measuring the same numbers on the same spreadsheets, and using the same tired management tactics. They can be very hard to tell apart.

Most of the leaders we all work with throughout our careers are only distinguished by a few degrees in the things they do and say. They are similar in many more ways than they are different. This is why exceptional leaders are so crucially important and memorable for the people they work with. The generic nature of most of today's leaders presents an excellent opportunity for a progressive person who is serious about developing his or her personal brand as a leader.

DEVELOPING YOUR PERSONAL BRAND

If this is something you have never thought much about, the best thing is to start with where you are. Remember, you don't have a choice about having a personal brand, you only have a choice about what it is. Let's start with this question:

What do you think your personal brand is today?

Try to think objectively about yourself and what you are known for to a certain group of people, maybe your team at work. Remember that your brand is the sum total of what people know and believe about you, combined with the feelings they get when they think about you. Our feelings about people are wired in such a way that we get a reaction without conscious thought.

That doesn't mean that one's brand can't change, it certainly can. What it means is that the thinking you will do about your own personal brand will be much deeper than anyone else will do when they think about you.

Want proof? Here is a list of unrelated names of people you probably have some impression about. This impression they have made on you is their brand image in your mind. They are all people you have probably never met, and there may be some you don't know much about, but as you scan the list you will experience a brand impression of each of them.

Write down the first word that comes to mind with each person. Ready? Here we go:

Serena Williams: _____

Mark Zuckerberg: _____

Derek Jeter: _____

Martha Stewart: _____

Axl Rose: _____

Alec Baldwin: _____

Miley Cyrus: _____

Jon Stewart: _____

John McCain: _____

Garth Brooks: _____

Lebron James: _____

Bill Gates: _____

Dwayne Johnson: _____

Kanye West: _____

Brad Pitt: _____

Carly Fiorina: _____

Tom Cruise: _____

Tiger Woods: _____

Arnold Schwarzenegger: _____

Brian Williams: _____

Next, look at your one-word descriptions and think about what you might have written five or ten years ago about the same person. Personal brands are dynamic and always in flux.

Your brand image of all of these people has everything to do with yourself. Your age, your politics, your tastes, your news sources, where you live, everything about you informs your perceptions. Looking back at the list you will see many people whose personal brands have changed drastically over the years that we have known of them.

Some of them have spent a lot of time (and money) trying to alter or rehabilitate their brands. This kind of change over time is called your Brand Story. Your personal brand is dynamic and in flux all of the time. It is much more like a movie than a picture. This is why it is so important to exert some deliberate control of it.

We would recommend that you actually write out what you think your brand is today. What you think you are known for, what people say about you, and how you are regarded. There are lots of ways to think about it, the best way is to keep it simple. Consider yourself in the third person, and be as objective as you can be about yourself.

Try your best to finish these prompts accurately:

_____ is seen as _____.

_____ is known for _____.

_____ has a reputation as a_____.

His/her peers would say he/she was _____.

His or her team would say _____.

His or her friends would say _____.

His or her neighbors would say _____.

None of these comments by themselves would accurately represent your personal brand, but the sum total of everyone's impressions and beliefs about you would. It can be hard to step outside of yourself and be objective. Many leaders we have worked with don't feel comfortable with their self-assessments. Many have asked colleagues and teammates these same kinds of questions to get a more accurate view of how they are seen by others.

Some progressive leaders have done formal 360-degree assessments to get a broad sample of anonymous opinions about themselves and their reputations with (1) people who report to them, (2) people they report to, and (3) colleagues at a peer level. Invariably, these leaders have been surprised at some of the responses. In most cases, the view they had of themselves did not line up exactly with their actual reputation with others. Sometimes the brand image that came into focus through this 360-degree view was much more negative or ambivalent than the leader expected

Exceptional leaders understand that purposeful development of their personal reputations and brands gives them an opportunity to deliver something different, progressive and meaningful in their role as leader. It should be understood that none of us can please everyone, and that's not at all the objective of developing your personal brand.

The bottom line: Purposeful development of your brand is a "must" for today's leaders. Let's move on to exactly how we can do that.

The One Thing: _____

_____

Playbook Notes: _____

_____

_____

_____

_____

> "Today you are you, that is truer than true.
> There is no one alive who is youer than you."
>
> **-Dr. Seuss**

THE SIX STEPS TO LEVERAGING YOUR PERSONAL BRAND

HOW DO YOU KNOW when it is time for active personal brand development? Let's take a test and see how you do. There are ten questions below that will help you know if your personal brand could use some polishing.

1. Do you hear yourself saying the same things?
2. Are you not being sought out as often for input or ideas?
3. Have you been in your role for more than five years?
4. Does it seem like you have less career momentum than you used to?
5. Do you frequently feel undervalued?
6. Have you worked with most of your team for more than five years?
7. Do you feel like you are going through the motions?

8. Are you not being invited to participate in new projects?

9. Have you had a change in your fitness, wardrobe or haircut in the last five years?

10. Are you the same predictable person?

Consider your answers to these questions. If the answer is "Yes" to more than three of them then it is time to start working deliberately on your personal brand. The good news is that it is possible to begin to positively develop your personal brand right away. There are six crucial steps to developing your personal brand, and you will want to spend some time with each of them. Remember, you don't get to decide if you have a personal brand or not... you do. What you can decide is that it's going to be an accurate reflection of how you want to be seen by the people that matter most to you.

Let's move on to the Six Steps:

IDENTIFY YOUR STRENGTHS

What are you great at? _____
_____

What are things you wish everyone knew about you? _____
_____

Are your strengths well known? _____

_____

What is your secret Superpower?_____

_____

*Your "Superpower" is a talent or ability that people have no idea about. It's not part of your job… but it could be.

WEAKEN YOUR WEAKNESSES

What are your skill-set weaknesses today? _____

_____

(Be absolutely objective)

What are you pretending is not important? _____

_____

Exactly what would it take to improve? _____

_____

DISCOVER YOUR DIFFERENTIATORS

Think about what makes you original and unique.

How are you different from your peer group? _____

_____

What traits make you unique? _____

_____

Personal Branding means being more "You" more of the time.

IDENTIFY YOUR PERSONAL BRAND UPSIDE (PBU)

Where can you get better fast?

_____

What are three priority improvement areas:

(1) _____

(2) _____

(3) _____

DEVELOP YOUR PERSONAL BRANDING BLUEPRINT (PBB)

-How would you really like to be known? _____

_____

-How would you benefit from these changes? _____

_____

START ACTING LIKE THE PERSON YOU WANT TO BE

What are some tangible first steps you can take right away?

_____

How can you make this version of you more visible to others?

_____

This is important, it is the **imprint you want to make on the world**.

> "Be yourself, everybody else is already taken."
>
> **– Oscar Wilde**

We have had Exceptional Leaders Lab workshop retreats where people spend a weekend going through these steps. They share their realizations and objectives with like-minded leaders, getting candid feedback from their peers. Lots of studies show that this kind of in-depth work is taken more seriously when people are working with a coach in person. Typically, introspective "self work" is not executed as successfully when someone is by themselves and working from a book. So, you may want to consider as a next step, attending a workshop or aligning with a coach for a period of time.

Here are the historical numbers:

About 1 in 5 people will take deliberate action after attending a workshop with a live coach. Only about 1 in 30 will take the same kind of deliberate action when they are working from a book by themselves. Here's the good news… the 1 out of 30 is just as likely to stick with and follow-through on the decisions they make as the 1 out of 5 with personal coaching. The recommendation? Be the "1" in the 1 out of 30, even if you need to bring in some help.

Developing your personal brand is as important as anything you will do in your professional lives. It is worth deliberate study, planning and follow-through. You do not want your personal brand to be an accident.

The One Thing: _____

_____

Playbook Notes: _____

_____

_____

_____

_____

> "Life isn't about finding yourself, life is about creating yourself."
>
> **-George Bernard Shaw**

ACTIVELY MANAGING YOUR PERSONAL BRAND

THIS LAST SECTION ON personal branding is where we will get strategic. As we have discussed, you personal brand is in your control. It is your responsibility. With that in mind, we need to be deliberate about managing our brands in the minds of the people who are most important in our lives.

Have you ever seen one of those amazing pictures where thousands of little photographs are put together in a collage to form one big picture, often of the same subject? Usually you can't even tell that the big picture is made of little pictures until you get very close to it. Why are we talking about this? Because this is exactly how your personal brand works. It is an aggregation of everyone's picture of you that forms the big picture of you.

The important difference is that some people's impressions of you will be decidedly more important than others. Your spouse, your friends, your kids, your boss, your peers... these are the impressions we all want to prioritize. These are the impressions we want to pay attention to and manage. We can trust that our friends and family will be patient with us through ups and downs. We expect them to love us, warts and all.

Can we count on that kind of patience at work? With our teams? With our peers? With the people we report to? Probably not. This is when we will need to be strategic and deliberate.

Let's start with a list of five people. First, list the five people with whom you need to have the best possible professional reputation and personal brand. These are the five people who will have the most influence over your career and responsibilities going forward:

1. _____ • _____
2. _____ • _____
3. _____ • _____
4. _____ • _____
5. _____ • _____

After you have made your list of the five people with whom your personal brand matters most, give yourself a letter grade that reflects how positive you believe your personal brand is with each person.

Add an A, B, C, D or F next to each name. An "A" would be someone who you know has a very high opinion of you, your skill set, and your ability to grow and perform. An "F" would reflect a relationship where the person you listed has a very low opinion of your skill set and low confidence in your ability to drive results. Most of your important relationship will be somewhere in between "A" and "F".

The next step in the strategic brand management process is to think through your relationships where you have the lowest grades. Typically, if you feel that your reputation/brand is low with an important person, it is. We are all a lot more likely to think we are seen positively than negatively. Therefore, negatively graded relationships represent important brand upside for you.

Let's focus on the two lowest grades, and do some thinking about them. This is the point where progressive thinking becomes progressive action. We'll add two more lines to each relationship, with some specific information to consider:

JOHN SULLIVAN • C

What part of your personal brand or reputation do you think this person sees negatively?

_____

What are some specific ways that you could begin to positively influence his perceptions of you?

_____

What personal win(s) can you help this person attain?

_____

MARTHA JACOBY • D

What part of your personal brand or reputation do you think this person sees negatively?

What are some specific ways that you could begin to positively influence her perceptions of you?

What personal win(s) can you help this person attain?

Thinking about these people in this way is the first step in gradually, and permanently, influencing their impression of you. You can't directly change someone's view of you, but you can certainly maintain an active awareness of relationships you need to improve.

It's very important to think through and be aware of the tangible ways you can positively influence their perceptions. With awareness, your relationship grade and value will absolutely grow over time. This is strategic personal brand management, and it's an important part of exceptional leadership.

The One Thing: _____

_____

Playbook Notes: _____

_____

_____

_____

_____

> "Great leaders don't necessarily set out to be a leader…
> they set out to make a difference. It's never about the role,
> and always about the goal."
>
> **-Lisa Haisha**

THE SIX BASELINE COMPETENCIES OF EXCEPTIONAL LEADERS

L EADING A TEAM is one of the most challenging jobs you can have. You must deal with many variables every single day to develop a team capable of performing at a consistently high level. Market forces, team attrition, competitive pressure, motivational challenges, personality issues, technical challenges, these are just some of the obstacles leaders must navigate through and around if they want to lead a truly excellent team.

There are six baseline competencies that almost all excellent leaders grasp and leverage to develop their teams. These are six key understandings that allow these leaders to seize growth opportunities and manage a dynamic team at a high level.

Let's summarize them here:

1. THEY KNOW THAT EXCEPTIONAL LEADERSHIP STARTS WITH TRULY EXCEPTIONAL LEADERS

Here is a sentence that only developed leaders will agree with: most of the upside on your team will come from what you can learn and execute as a leader. Underperforming leaders always seem to believe that growth depends on external and less managable factors. These are factors like recruiting, the economy, competitors, product pricing and positioning, compensation, etc.

Do these things matter? Of course. Are they the difference between the average and the amazing leader? Absolutely not. Exceptional leaders go to work on themselves first. They are constantly expanding their skills sets, their leadership vocabulary, and their expectations for what a high-performing team really is.

2. THEY KNOW THAT COACHING BEATS MANAGING

Excellent leaders get it. They know that a coach who is engaged every day in what their team is actually doing to win business will always outperform a manager who leads from behind their desk, by trying to drive activity with spreadsheets, manipulations and the "metrics".

3. THEY'RE NOT STUCK IN A TIME CAPSULE

Today's exceptional leaders are dynamic and progressive. They are leaning in and leveraging any new tool, tactic, technology or technique they can use to drive results. They are not doing their job the exact same way they did five or ten years ago. Obsolescence will not find them, they are moving too fast.

4. THEY UNDERSTAND THE DIFFERENCE BETWEEN MIRRORS AND WINDOWS

Average leaders always seem to be looking out the window to see where growth opportunities are going to come from. Is there a better person out there? Is there a shortcut? Excellent leaders look directly in the mirror for growth. They ask: what can I do? What can I learn? How can I better influence my team?

5. THEY KNOW THAT "CULTURE EATS STRATEGY FOR BREAKFAST"

This is management author and expert Peter Drucker's most famous quote for a reason; it is undeniably true. Today's progressive leaders understand the force of culture in an organization. It is the most powerful and potent competitive advantage a leader can develop. It's what makes people want to come to… and stay with… your team. It is why you don't have to have industry-leading compensation or the best location. It is why it doesn't even really matter what your company does, because culture can be grown anywhere. Your organization's culture is its upside or its biggest risk.

6. THEY LEAD BY EXAMPLE

Could this really be the most powerful secret of excellent leaders? Yes, it could. Exceptional leaders lead from the front. They use their own personal activity and priorities to drive the activity and priorities of their teams. The leader sets the pace for learning with a high-energy approach to their work. This creates an "excuse proof" work environment that attracts high performers and repels pretenders, which is exactly what they want.

Those are the six baseline understandings of exceptional leaders. These ideas will be knit into other topics throughout the book. Think about how each one applies to you. Is there an aspect of your leadership you could improve? Do you have untapped upside as a leader that is apparent in one of these ideas? We bet you do.

The One Thing: _____

_____

Playbook Notes: _____

_____

_____

_____

_____

> "If we are growing, we are always going to be
> out of our comfort zone."
>
> **-John Maxwell**

UNDERSTANDING YOUR COACHING PERSONALITY

EVERY LEADER IS different, and we all bring different strengths and weaknesses to work with us. The ability to objectively (and accurately) understand how our personality affects our coaching is a key component of improving as a leader.

We need to know exactly what we're working with before areas of opportunity will come into focus. Remember, coaching is leadership in action. We will use both words in describing how these key personality traits come together for all of us.

After working with hundreds of leaders and organizations we developed what we now call the ACCESS coaching personality matrix. We realized that there is a "recipe" to leaders' personalities and every leader has different amounts of individual ingredients that come together to form their full personality. Wherever you work, regardless of industry, location, or the size of your organization, you will find the same leadership personality traits.

These are the characteristics that make up the overall population of leaders everywhere. This mix of traits is how you are presenting yourself as a coach to the people on your team. These are the traits that are either adding to… or subtracting from… your overall influence.

Your coaching personality matrix is made up of six main personality variables. How you are perceived as a coach can be understood as a unique combination of these factors. Leadership personalities are constructed around leaders that have similar weights and strengths in the six factors, but every leader is original and unique in some key ways. Here they are the personality variables:

Ambition

Credibility

Competency

Expressiveness

Sensitivity

Self-Awareness

Think of these six factors as the "recipe" of your coaching personality. If they were going to make another you, they would have to stir in different amounts of the ingredients above. These are the pieces that come together to form your coaching personality. You can remember the six factors with the acronym A.C.C.E.S.S. Let's review them and see how you see yourself.

AMBITION

Ambition is often misconstrued as a negative trait. People are often described as being too ambitious, especially as leaders, and it can lead to distrust. That's not a true or fair understanding of ambition. Ambition is fuel, and it is as simple as that. Does a leader have enough "ambition fuel" to do the things that need to be done? Does the leader have enough ambition to learn new things so they can improve their performance? Is the leader ambitious enough to want to be exceptional in their role?

Ambition makes people go. It is an extension of a person's self-esteem and answers the question; what does this leader expect from him or herself?

CREDIBILITY

This word is often misused. Credibility is not how well you do your job or know your stuff… that is Competence. Credibility is how well people think you know your stuff. Credibility is built on perception and reputation. Competence is built on actual ability. Credibility is a huge factor in being a successful coach, especially when the leader is working with a new team. How would you rate your overall level of credibility in the eyes of the people you lead? How do you see your credibility in the eye of the people you report to?

COMPETENCE

Competence is just old-fashioned "know how". Someone's level of competence is exactly equal to their ability to understand or execute a specific job or task. Competence is a fascinating concept because of how we are all highly competent in some areas and completely incompetent in others.

We're all constructed with a particular mix of competency levels in every area of our life. This gives us an objective sensitivity to people who don't know how to do certain things. It keeps us relevant. It also allows us to recognize false competence almost immediately. As leaders, there are specific things we must know how to do. Final thought: You can fake credibility temporarily, but you can't fake competence at all.

EXPRESSIVENESS

Here is where many leaders are drastically under-developed. They are competent managers, they know what needs to be happening with the people on their teams, but they just don't know the most effective ways to get their message across. Because of this, whatever level of competence they have achieved is blunted and muted. Expressiveness covers a lot of bases. It includes communication skills (verbal & written), emotion, body language, passion, charisma and their leadership vocabulary.

For most leaders, specific kinds of expressiveness are crucially important to their influence and success. This could be conference call skills, public speaking skills, webinar expressiveness, one-on-one expressiveness or boardroom skills. Whatever kind of expressiveness is important in your leadership role, you must master it to be able to optimize the other five parts of your leadership personality.

SENSITIVITY

This may be the least "learnable" of the six parts of leader's personality. Sensitivity is the leader's ability to feel what is happening with a person or a group. The most effective leaders can sense the energy in people and know when is the right time to say and do certain things. Empathy, also a key leadership trait... can be defined as sympathy in action.

Sometimes it is timely sympathy, sometimes it can be the moment for an empathetic response, most of the time it is just having a good sense of timing and paying attention.

Sensitivity to other personalities is also crucial to a leaders success. We have all experienced the cringe that comes when a leader says the wrong thing (competence) at the wrong time (sensitivity) in the wrong way (expressiveness). We have all seen a leader "lose the room" with an insensitive remark or a topic that is not suited to the audience. The main problem with the insensitive leader is that they almost always think that the problem is the audience. It is a classic "they don't know what they don't know" scenario. Which brings us to the sixth and last part of the leader's personality recipe...

SELF-AWARENESS

Nothing will affect a leader's overall effectiveness more than a lack of self-awareness. This particular part of the leader's personality also changes more over time than any other of the six parts. Most us probably start our careers with too much self-awareness. We think about how we look, how we sound, how we are being perceived. It's possible to think about perception more than authenticity, and some of us are guilty of it. Usually this is just a temporary developmental stage for new leaders.

What happens over time with many successful leaders is just the opposite of that. As they experience success in their roles and rise within their organizations, their self-awareness starts to recede.

They are getting less constructive criticism. They are doing the performance reviews now, and not getting reviewed themselves.

Here's where things go wrong; this leader can now convince themselves that their ideas are always the best, and that the care they once took in their communications and relationships doesn't matter as much anymore. It is almost a business cliché, the President, VP or CEO with little or no self-awareness. They can actually get to the point where they can no longer learn and no longer be coached. We've seen it first-hand many times, maybe you have too.

The bottom line is all learning leaders need to actively maintain their humility. Surprisingly, the personality trait of humility along with a healthy level of self-awareness will make you the most effective leader you can be. You will see what people need and what they expect, and you will know exactly how you can get better. We'll spend more time on the power of humility later.

So those are the six pieces of the leadership personality puzzle. How they come together forms your leadership matrix.

Take a minute and give your self a score of 1-10 based on your strength in each of the six ACCESS personality areas. Give yourself a 10 if you are very strong in one area and a 1 if it is a very weak area. This will help you be more aware of sections of the book that talk directly to an upside area for you.

| **Ambition** | 1 – 2 – 3 – 4 – 5 – 6 – 7 – 8 – 9 – 10 |
| **Credibility** | 1 – 2 – 3 – 4 – 5 – 6 – 7 – 8 – 9 – 10 |

Competence	1 – 2 – 3 – 4 – 5 – 6 – 7 – 8 – 9 – 10
Expressiveness	1 – 2 – 3 – 4 – 5 – 6 – 7 – 8 – 9 – 10
Sensitivity	1 – 2 – 3 – 4 – 5 – 6 – 7 – 8 – 9 – 10
Self-Awareness	1 – 2 – 3 – 4 – 5 – 6 – 7 – 8 – 9 – 10

Make a mental note of your strongest and weakest areas above. Most leaders will use their strongest trait in the matrix to offset their weakest. Take another look at your strongest and weakest areas, you'll probably see that this is true for you too. This is a form of compensation that's not a good substitute for actually improving the area where you are weakest. In fact, your weakest trait is your real leadership upside.

There are two outward-facing attributes in the matrix, expressiveness and sensitivity. These two traits have a strong impact on how your other four traits are experienced by your team. It's important to notice if you rated yourself low in those two areas, as it may have something to do with influence gaps you may discern with people on your team

Remember that every one of us is original and unique based both on the strong and weak parts of our personality. The great news is that all six of these variables can be strongly influenced. The key to influencing these traits is in understanding that you can improve; believing that you are not a finished product gives any learning leader a lot of exciting upside.

The One Thing: _____

_____

Playbook Notes: _____

_____

_____

_____

_____

> "Only three things happen naturally in organizations; friction, confusion and underperformance. Everything else requires leadership."
>
> **-Peter Drucker**

HOW EXCEPTIONAL LEADERS MANAGE STRESS

MANAGING STRESS IS **critical for leaders.** You don't have the luxury of being grumpy, absent, irritable or volatile. Those are indulgences that you can no longer claim when you have high expectations for yourself and others. Many people will never become truly effective in their leadership roles, because they can't hold themselves together well enough to perform at a consistently high level.

Everyone understands that it isn't possible to eliminate stress from your world, so the only constructive way to approach the topic is to examine where your personal stress comes from and then reflect on ways to manage it. For most people, stress comes from three distinct sources. Studying these sources is the first step in learning how to deal with it positively. For most of us, simply figuring out where your personal stress is coming from helps us to manage it. The experts tell us that a feeling of control over daily pressure and stress is rooted in an understanding of ourselves, and how clearly we understand our stressors.

In the study of personality psychology, "locus of control" is a term that describes the extent to which individuals believe they can control events that affect them. Individuals with a high internal locus of control believe that events in their life derive primarily from their own actions. For example, when receiving test results, people with an internal locus of control tend to praise or blame themselves and their abilities, whereas people with an external locus of control tend to praise or blame an external factor such as the teacher or the test.

With salespeople, the "internal" people will believe that they can control outcomes based on their preparation, their enthusiasm and their closing skills. The "external" people will believe that the success of the presentation has to do with the mood of the prospect, the materials provided by the marketing department, the approved pricing, etc.

EXTERNAL LOCUS OF CONTROL PEOPLE

Having an external locus of control describes a person who looks outward for approval and recognition. This person may be a very capable person in every way and who, over time, may develop a need for outside approval in order to feel good about himself or the job he's doing. This person generally works very well in group or team environments and can be an excellent collaborator. He's coachable and respectful of the "chain of command" in the organization.

INTERNAL LOCUS OF CONTROL PEOPLE

Having an "internal" locus of control means that the person's sense of accomplishment, success, and capability comes from the inside. These people tend to be wary of lots of positive recognition and are not always the best collaborators. They're usually good organizers and successful lead-from-the-front managers where their credibility can be seen clearly.

Many leaders develop an "external" locus of control over time because they need to satisfy so many people. This is where having an external locus of control can make it hard to become an exceptional leader. When you consider the leader's need to be sensitive to his team, to perform for his bosses, to be attentive to his partner, and to have quality time with his kids, it's easy to see where the stress would come from.

It can be very challenging keeping all of these different people satisfied. Because of this, many leaders begin to feel good about themselves to the extent that they can please others, thus, an external locus of control.

A good way to discern how people are psychologically constructed is to ask the simple question, "How do you know when you've done a good job?" Their first responses will indicate an internal or external locus of control. If they say, "I know because I feel good about myself," or, "I feel proud to have accomplished something," they're self-satisfiers who are able to feel successful without other people telling them they're successful. On the contrary, if the question is answered with something like, "When my boss is impressed," or, "I get recognized," or "I earn my bonus," then you know they want the outside world to tell them they're successful.

Top performing people need to be careful with this because either extreme can cause problems. Think about where your personal locus of control is. Is this way of thinking helping you as a leader? Is it something you may need to try and change over time? Top performers need to understand that most of the improvement they make will happen on the inside, and be reflected and magnified in their relationships with people. They are not afraid to examine themselves and look for areas they could improve, and this trait gives them ultimate credibility with their teams and peers.

What are some other stressors that can affect our ability to lead successfully?

NOT LIVING UP TO YOUR POTENTIAL

Another big source of stress among high achievers and leaders is the idea that they're doing less than they can or should. Most leaders consider themselves to be highly capable performers who can produce at a high level all of the time but, realistically, this is almost impossible to do. Many leaders put intense pressure on themselves to perform at an incredibly high level all of the time without making any compromises. It's this prototypical highly ambitious, competitive type-A individual who's most likely to experience the kind of stress that comes from being unrealistic about his capability.

A person can't be "on" all of the time, and it's not even in a person's best interest to try. Success is about balance and knowing when it's time to turn things up and when it's time to use the brakes. Deliberately slowing yourself down can be one of the hardest things to do.

We must understand that every meeting is not "the" meeting, every month is not "the" month, and every presentation is not "the" presentation. Top performers have real perspective and learn that the ability to demonstrate a balanced approach is as important for their followers as it is for themselves.

As a high-performance person, you have a thousand little "moments of truth" each week and it's important to be able to differentiate them. Listed below are a few areas of confusion that can knock an otherwise capable leader out of balance if he doesn't know the difference between:

» Busyness and productivity

» Hard work and performance

» Completion and accomplishment

» Being highly motivated and being hyperactive

People probably depend on you to model both goal-orientation and balance. Sometimes, that means pulling back on the accelerator a bit. Allow yourself to do this and your team's overall performance will increase while your personal stress level decreases. Another benefit: when a leader can make things look easy they always have more success developing other leaders.

THINKING ABOUT YOURSELF TOO MUCH

"The greatest cause of stress is thinking about yourself to much." I remember where I was the first time I heard that sentence. It was at a leadership seminar outside of Atlanta in the mid-1990s. The topic under discussion was stress and where it comes from. I didn't accept this statement at first. I simply wrote it in my journal to consider later. I've thought about it many times since then, and I eventually realized that it's absolutely true. It's become almost fashionable to be "stressed out" and to say how busy you are when someone asks you how you're doing.

Why isn't being calm, peaceful, and serene fashionable? It should be. Instead, everyone wants to claim that they're busy and stressed. As a leader you have to think clearly about what's actually going on. It's true, stress is caused by overthinking about one's self.

Perhaps things aren't going the way you hoped they would go, you have not had enough time to do something you want to do, you're stressed because the month is looking bad, etc. A leader cannot get tangled up in this kind of thought and still be responsive to his team and his family.

One of our associates, Michael Brothers, recommends "starting at death and working backwards" to get an accurate read on how big a worry really is. If you compare your current worry level to the biggest worries possible, you will get some instant perspective on your situation and to remove some of the emotion from your thought process. Whatever coping mechanism you use, it's important to understand that simple, old-fashioned worry is the biggest root of most stress, both justifiable worry and fictional worry about things that will never happen.

Earl Nightingale said, "Worry is the misuse of the imagination." I believe that most stress could fall under that same definition. The best way to escape from self-centered stress is to get busy doing things for other people. Actively seek out people in your organization to help and teach, pulling your attention off of your own condition.

Feeling and expressing stress are not going to help anything anyway. We all have legitimate worries that should be taken seriously, but the rest of what we call stress is just noise and it's not going to go away. The best course of action may be to make a positive impact on as many people as you can. If we can do this, at least the noise will be much harder to hear.

The One Thing: _____

_____

Playbook Notes: _____

_____

_____

_____

> "Everything is energy and that's all there is to it. Match the frequency of the reality you want and you cannot help but get that reality. This is not philosophy, this is physics".
> **-Albert Einstein**

YOUR LEADERSHIP ENERGY AUDIT

ENERGY IS ONE OF your most crucial assets. What makes it especially important for leaders is that it dictates how you can deploy your other leadership assets. Your intellect, your attention, your sensitivity, your ability to listen and understand, your patience… these are all subject to your energy level. It could be said that personal energy is what fuels exceptional leadership. Low energy leaders, even very skilled ones, have trouble sustaining their influence.

The other consideration is your home life. Many leaders go home to their partners and families 100% spent. They have used up all of their patience, enthusiasm and sensitivity at work, and now there is nothing left for the people who really love them. With this in mind, energy management is a crucial quality of life issue. Bottom line: it's important.

An energy audit is a great way to look at this critical asset objectively. In most cases, taking a closer look at how your energy is accumulated and spent will inspire a progressive leader to make some adjustments. Activity, interaction and schedule adjustments can really pay off. We'll look at both of our energy opportunities: adding more energy to our lives; and, managing some of the big energy stealers we are dealing with.

There are five steps to an effective energy audit. Let's gets started:

Step One – Make a list of things that give you energy. Anything can go on this list: for some people it is exercise or a hobby. For others it is solitude or social time. It may be a good night's sleep or getting up early. It can be a diversion like a book, going to the movies, going "screen-less" for a while or changing your daily routine. It may be time with a certain person or group. Lots of things can energize a person. Think deeply and make a list.

_____

_____

_____

_____

_____

Step Two – Make a list of things that reduce your energy level. This can be anything where there is a definite subtraction of your personal energy. For some people this may be travel, or their commute. It can be certain people, tasks or recurring meetings. Lot's of things use up energy. List the things that eat up the most personal energy for you.

_____

_____

_____

_____

_____

_____

_____

Step Three – Now it's time to start looking critically at the things that may be stealing our energy. Leaders need to think about return on investment when it comes to their personal energy. We all have activities, routines and relationships where the ROI is very poor. These are unsustainable, if we want to continue growing our capability as leaders.

We recommend categorizing your big energy spends in a way that will surface opportunities to preserve energy. There are four categories that you can remember with the acronym "REDS". The categories are: Reduce, Eliminate, Delegate and Structure.

Leaders can preserve a considerable amount of energy by being deliberate in how they spend it. Energy is just like money, you have to be careful about how it's being spent or it will affect your lifestyle and general happiness. Go back to your list in Step Two and see if you can apply one of the REDS categories to some of your big energy spends.

> » Can you **Reduce** the amount of time you spend doing something?
> » Can you **Eliminate** one of your big energy spends?
> » Is there anything you can **Delegate**?
> » Do you have anything listed that you can **Structure** differently?

Add an R, E, D or S where you see an opportunity on your Step Two list.

Step Four – Now, we're going to revisit your list of things that give you energy from your list in Step One. Look closely at your list and circle or highlight the things that you could easily do more of. It may be an activity or routine. It may be more time with a certain person or more time alone. It may be an exercise or dietary change. You can't do more of everything, just choose a few items that you definitely can increase to add more energy to your life.

Step Five – Now it's time to make our short-term energy enhancement plan. It may turn out to be a long-term plan, but some of these changes won't be easy, so we'll take baby steps to insure success. You want a simple energy growth and enhancement plan that is easy to start and possible to maintain. You will have setbacks, just like with any other important change, but the payoff can be huge.

The plan is a potent combination of energy-increasers and energy-savers that will combine to produce results that can increase your overall energy on day one. Here's our recommendation:

Take three of your energy increasers from the first list and knit them into your schedule. If possible, work all of your top three into your weekly schedule, either during the workweek or the weekend. Important: they need to actually be scheduled, and not just be a to-do list. Add them to your planner or Outlook calendar. They are appointments.

1. Schedule _____

2. Schedule _____

3. Schedule _____

Next we'll leverage your energy-reducer list. You should consider everything on this list to be an "energy risk". This means that those activities, routines and people are making energy withdrawals that may be affecting other parts of your personal or professional life.

Using the REDS categories, pick one thing from your Energy Reducers list that you can manage in each way. It's important to pick just one from each category so you can experience immediate success managing low-ROI activities.

Reduce _____

Eliminate _____

Delegate _____

Structure _____

Congratulations! You have completed the leadership energy audit and organized a plan to add more energy to your life while reducing low-ROI activities and interactions. Work your plan for a few weeks and then make any needed adjustments. You are now actively managing your most valuable asset, your energy.

The One Thing: _____

_____

Playbook Notes: _____

_____

_____

_____

_____

> "Your energy introduces you before you even speak."
>
> **-Patrick Consing**

THE DYNAMIC DOZEN + ONE:

13 GREAT WAYS TO SUSTAIN YOUR PERSONAL ENERGY

THE ABILITY TO SUSTAIN a high level of energy through the workday is a crucial attribute of successful leaders. There are many people who are talented and smart who are not as effective as they could be because they haven't worked on this important part of their professional skill set. Maybe you have worked with people like this, very bright folks who get irritable, less creative or mentally slower during certain parts of the day.

They are still capable people, of course, but their body and mind are undermining their performance. We have all experienced the feeling of low energy at work, we know we are not at our best, and sometimes we're just going through the motions. This is just not an option for high-performance leaders, so it makes sense to learn how to sustain a level of energy that will allow you to be at your best most of the time.

Take a minute and think through your energy ups and downs during a workday or workweek. We all have energy patterns that tend to repeat based on our habits and routines. Your energy level, whether it is high or low at a certain time, is the result of your routines. It can definitely be changed and altered if your energy is dipping during the wrong times. Here are some questions to help you consider your own energy patterns:

> » I am most creative in the morning, mid-day, afternoon, or evening.

> » I can get grouchy in the morning, mid-day, afternoon or evening.

> » I am likely to have good ideas _____.

> » The most stressful part of my week is _____.

> » The meeting I look forward to least is _____.

> » The meeting I look forward to most is _____.

> » After lunch I feel _____.

> » My energy level seems to be highest during this part of the day: _____

> » When I get home after work I feel:_____

Now that you have thought through your energy ebbs and flows throughout the week it will be easier to see where the "soft spots" are in your routine. This makes it easier to make high impact adjustments.

What follows is a list of recommendations that can help you preserve and sustain your energy throughout the day. All twelve of these recommendations are real-world proven and can absolutely affect how you go through your work day. There are probably a few of these ideas that you are using already, our hope is that you can utilize one or more of the following recommendations as leverage to increase your energy while you work. Ready? Let's get started!

RECOMMENDATION #1 – START YOUR DAY EARLY

This is probably the last thing that many of you want to do, as not everyone is a "morning person". As an energy preserver, getting an early start is crucial. It allows a person to calmly ramp into their day before they have to start reacting to things. Starting the day early means you begin each day on your terms, working on your priorities instead of other people's. If you're not a morning person, it is especially important to allow yourself at least 30 minutes before the official start to your day to give yourself a chance to "lean in" to each new day.

RECOMMENDATION #2 – MANAGE YOUR MEETINGS TO PRESERVE ENERGY

One of the easiest ways to preserve energy through the day is to have unscheduled space in between meetings and other responsibilities. Just a little time between scheduled responsibilities can make a big difference in your ability to "change channels" and be ready for whatever comes next. Towards that end, We strongly recommend that scheduled meetings and conference calls end 10 minutes before the hour or half-hour. For example, a previously hour-long meeting starting at 2:00 would be scheduled to end at 2:50. That way, even if another meeting starts at 3:00 you can clear your mind and be ready for a new topic and new attendees.

RECOMMENDATION #3 – HAVE TWO DIFFERENT WEB BROWSERS FOR WORK & PERSONAL SITES

One of the biggest distractions and energy-eaters for today's workers is the internet. Your personal sites for social networking, etc. are constantly on your screen begging for your attention. Having two browsers is a simple way to keep your mind on work while you are working, and off work when you are not. Keep your personal bookmarks on one browser and your work site bookmarked on the other. Voila'… you just saved five hours a week and kept your mind fresh for whatever you are working on.

RECOMMENDATION #4 - CONSIDER A STAND-UP DESK

There are a lot of experts who tout the positive effects stand-up desks have on circulation and back pain, but this recommendation is all about sustaining energy. Standing up at your desk for some part of the day… even if it is just an hour or two… can make a huge difference in your energy level through the day. Some people set a timer for their standing time, other stand for a while after lunch, and others stand all day. Stand-up desks have dropped in price over the last couple of years and sellers like NextDesk, VariDesk, Rebel Desk, Up-Lift and Stand Desk all offer desks in prices ranging from $500-$2500. Most of these are adjustable so they can work as both traditional seated desks and standing desks.

RECOMMENDATION #5 – START YOUR DAY WITH SOMETHING OTHER THAN EMAIL

This simple recommendation can make a big difference in how the workday gets going for you. It is easy to feel overwhelmed when you look at your inbox, especially if you work in a time zone where your co-workers are starting their days before you. Try doing something else… anything else… other than looking at email first thing in the morning: plan for your day, read a book or blog with your coffee, take a short walk, do some stretching, eat breakfast… you get the idea. You will be looking at your email all day long, there is no reason to rush to it first thing.

RECOMMENDATION #6 – LIMIT MULTI-TASKING

It feels like you are saving time when you multi-task, but current research is starting to show that you are just doing things a little worse… two or three things at a time. Experts recommend a sequenced approach to doing tasks, that we focus on what we are doing while we are doing it. Part of being focused is just not being distracted. Sometimes that might mean participating on a conference call away from your computer, reviewing a report with your phone turned off or leveraging recommendation #3 above.

RECOMMENDATION #7 – WATCH THE "CC" LINE ON EMAIL MESSAGES

The "CC" line can be an energy eater and a time waster. If you are included in too many messages where you are not central to the theme or purpose, start aggressively deleting them and consider asking to be dropped from the thread if other people are driving the issue. When you are composing email, be very discerning about who you add to the message. Every person included increases the odds of more email being generated, and each thread participant dilutes the clarity of who is responsible for responding to the message or dealing with the issue at hand.

RECOMMENDATION #8 – LIMIT YOUR TIME WITH TOXIC PEOPLE

We all have people in our lives that take a lot more than they give. Unfortunately we don't always get to choose who we have in our lives, but when we do we need to be very deliberate. High-energy leaders are careful to make sure they have a lot more "plus" people than "minus" people in their personal and professional circles. Often you can improve the quality of your interactions with someone when you need or want to. Other times it's better to let a relationship fade away. We are talking about all kinds of relationships; associates, friends, family, social network connections, peers, neighbors, etc. It is amazing how much you can improve the net positive/negative level of your daily life by being deliberate in this area.

RECOMMENDATION #9 – BLOCK YOUR SCHEDULE TO ALLOW FOR DEVELOPMENTAL TIME

The idea is to actually schedule blank time in your weekly schedule for the development of projects, research, personal brainstorming, prioritizing and organizations. You should treat this time just like you would any other appointment in your schedule. An hour a day is the ideal amount of time to devote to "blank" time. If you absolutely are not able to find that hour then any amount will help you sustain your energy through the day and week.

RECOMMENDATION #10 – EAT HEALTHY SNACKS & DRINK WATER THROUGH THE DAY

Do we sound like your Mother? It is true that eating healthy snacks like nuts and raw vegetables during the day will help sustain your energy and keep your metabolism up. Drinking water has all kinds of positive effects as we all know. Keep those healthy snacks and your extra-large water bottle close at hand and you will definitely feel an increase in your late-morning and late-afternoon energy level.

RECOMMENDATION #11 – ANSWER SOME EMAIL MESSAGES WITH A CALL

Going "old school" with your responses can help sustain your energy and save a lot of time in the process. When you get an email that requires a thoughtful response, pick up the phone and talk it through with the sender. Conversations are energizers, and you are likely to resolve an issue much faster than through a series of email messages.

RECOMMENDATION #12 – TAKE A 15-20 MINUTE SIESTA

You are going to like this one! Productivity experts have long espoused the value and impact of a short "power nap" each day. We know that many cultures have these organized rest periods built into their workdays. If you are not lucky enough to live in one of these cultures, you will need to be creative and deliberate to work this habit into your day. Of course, there will be many of us who will need to wait until after work to get our siesta in.

RECOMMENDATION #13 – START WITH YOUR TOP FIVE EVERY DAY

This recommendation is the oldest and probably the best idea for productivity and energy preservation. You start your day with the five most important things you need to accomplish that day.

Why five? It seems to be the magic number. If you can't get to the five most important things, you will certainly not get to number eight or number eleven. Hopping from thing to thing because you don't have a priority list is a big-time energy eater. The Top Five list will keep you focused on your key priorities and protect you from allowing other things to jump in front of your most important priorities.

That's the dynamic dozen plus one recommendations for preserving leadership energy. After you have thought through the list, pick out one or two of the recommendations that you think might have an impact in your life. We would encourage you to try any recommendation for a couple of weeks before you add another one; then you can make a decision about the next step you might take to upgrade your energy level. Energy preservation is a crucial part of being an exceptional leader; make it a priority.

The Dynamic Dozen + One:

The One Thing: _____

_____

Playbook Notes: _____

_____

_____

_____

> "Until you can make the unconscious conscious,
> it will direct your life… and you will call it fate".
>
> **-Carl Jung**

CRACKING THE CODE: HOW LEADERS GET BETTER

THE STUDY OF LEADERSHIP skill and competency is complicated. Leaders and coaches develop in a lot of different ways, and some of the ways we improve in other areas of our lives simply don't work in our leadership roles.

One example of this is leadership experience. The amount of experience someone has in leadership or coaching roles has very little to do with how effective that person actually is in their leadership. Remember, leadership is a verb, it is something you do. A promotion or a title can make you a leader, but it certainly doesn't make you good at it.

In our experience working with hundreds of leaders everywhere and of every type, we have discovered that simple leadership experience is not an indicator of skill or effectiveness. In fact, lots of experience in a leadership role can actually be a negative because (1) the leader may be overconfident in their skill because of their experience, and (2) their weaknesses and limitations will be well known by their team.

Exceptional leaders think of leadership as a craft. They know they will always be working to improve, and that what worked today may not work tomorrow.

There is a coaching slogan that says that "practice doesn't make perfect, it makes permanent". Only perfect practice makes for perfect execution. This is extremely applicable to leadership because so many leaders believe that it's their level of experience that makes them effective. Of course, that's only true if you have been doing the right things as a leader. Have you ever worked with a leader or manager who has done something the wrong way for a decade or more? We sure have. A poor reaction, recommendation or execution repeated for ten years straight is actually much more risky and dangerous than the same mistake made by a rookie manager.

Golf is a great example of how lots of wrongs can never end up as a right. Lots of people are passionate about golf, and that passion leads to a lot of enthusiasm and practice. On any golf range in the world you will see the same thing, avid golfers hitting hundreds of balls trying to get better. The problem is that most of them are practicing the exact swing that is keeping them from improving.

Again, and again, and again; they are cementing the poor mechanics that have caused the results they are trying to improve.

It's easy to see the analogy with leaders who have been in their role for a long time, becoming ever more confident using tactics and skills that may not work at all.

So how do leaders get better in their craft? How do they continue to develop themselves and their leadership skill sets? It all starts with intention. A leader who has the self-awareness to know that they can improve is a progressive leader. They know that they themselves are the leading indicator for the growth and performance of their organizations. Making the decision to spend some time with a book like this puts you in a special category; you are a leader who knows you have upside potential and have made a decision to exploit it.

One of the best ways to understand how leadership expertise actually develops is through the competency ladder described as the "Four Stages of Learning Any New Skill" by Noel Burch in the early 1970's. It is the best way of understanding how we can purposefully improve our skills and effectiveness as leaders.

Let's do a quick review of the four stages:

Stage 1: **Unconsciously Incompetent** = I don't know that I don't know.

Stage 2: **Consciously Incompetent** = I now know that I don't know.

Stage 3: **Consciously Competent** = I know, but it takes a lot of concentration.

Stage 4: **Unconsciously Competent** = I automatically know, it's second nature.

Do you remember what it was like the first time you rode a bike? Before you were even aware bikes existed, you were at stage one. You were unconsciously incompetent. You had no idea about bikes, or your lack of ability to ride one. The moment you sat on the bike and attempted to ride it, you entered stage two. You became consciously incompetent. Stage two is tough for people because you realize you're not good at something. Most people try to avoid this stage because it is uncomfortable not knowing how to execute something. This is where fear really keeps most people from even attempting new things.

With a little bit of time and practice, you finally hit stage three, you were consciously competent. You knew how to ride, and you could ride without training wheels or help, but you really had to think about it. You were riding the bike with a fake smile while white-knuckling the handlebars. Then you hit stage four, which is unconsciously competent. You could ride without any conscious thought about how to ride a bike.

We are all at stage four with many things that happen every day. Breathing, walking, eating, talking, driving and perhaps even in how we treat people.

In order to make sure you're distinguishing the stages of competency, take a minute to think of one personal example you have in each of the four stages. You will find it hardest to think of a personal example in the unconsciously incompetent category. This is because these are topics, skills, and knowledge outside of your current awareness.

I'll share one surprising skill I realized where I was Unconsciously Incompetent just a few months ago. It was even more basic than riding a bike, and I was stunned to realize that I didn't know how to do it right. The skill? Tying my shoelaces. That's right, I had been Unconsciously Incompetent at tying my shoes, and I'll bet you are too. Here's how I learned that "I didn't know that I didn't know" about how to tie my shoelaces.

A friend had watched a TED talk on tying shoe laces and forwarded it along. My wife and I watched it and learned a dramatically improved way to do it. Remember, we both had 40+ years of experience tying our shoes. We thought were unconsciously competent at this skill and it turned out that we were actually both unconsciously incompetent. We didn't know that we didn't know. The new way was MUCH better and it was very easy to learn. Your laces will stay horizontal on your shoe and look better, and they will never (that's right, never) come undone. Google it: TED talk shoe laces.

The lesson here is that if we can find a way to improve something as basic as that, just imagine all of the ways we can all improve something as complex, challenging and dynamic as leadership!

Now try to think of at least one personal example in each category.

Stage 1: **Unconsciously Incompetent** – <u>An example is not possible here</u>

Stage 2: **Consciously Incompetent** - _____

Stage 3: **Consciously Competent** - _____

Stage 4: **Unconsciously Competent** - _____

We want to share a few specific leadership examples for each level in the competency ladder. Each of these are examples that we've seen in leaders we have worked with. You may recognize a few of these traits.

STAGE 1 EXAMPLES: UNCONSCIOUSLY INCOMPETENT LEADERSHIP

These are real-world examples and scenarios where leaders are completely out of touch with what they should and could be doing in certain situations. This is by far the most challenging stage, because you don't know that you don't know.

» Not considering the audience in communications

» Missing great recognition opportunities

» Not recognizing obviously toxic people

» "Losing the room" in situations where influence is needed

» Poor grammar or vocabulary

» Bringing old skills into new situations

STAGE 2 EXAMPLES: CONSCIOUSLY INCOMPETENT LEADERSHIP

These are typical situations where a leader knows they are not fully competent. They find themselves "out of their depth" and realize they have a skill or knowledge shortfall. It is an uncomfortable feeling, and we have all had it.

» One-on-one conversations about serious personnel issues

» Situations requiring specific technical knowledge

» Situations where study or research was needed and not done

» Misunderstanding the personalities/temperaments involved in a situation

» Overestimating your own ability to persuade a person or group

STAGE 3 EXAMPLES: CONSCIOUSLY COMPETENT LEADERSHIP

This may be the biggest category for progressive leaders. These are situations where preparation and experience can drive successful leadership. Note: people in this category are the best trainers and coaches for these skills. They are succeeding at something new, but the skill or tactic is not yet automatic for them. That's the perfect profile for a successful teacher.

» Successfully building a consensus on an important decision

» Coaching a person towards a specific action or decision

» Organizing a plan or initiative for your organization

» Consciously recognizing good work and/or important progress

» Paying attention to individuals with clear upside

STAGE 4 EXAMPLES: UNCONSCIOUSLY COMPETENT LEADERSHIP

A lot of what leaders do in this stage has become instinct because of study and successful repetition. These actions are automatic. The leader knows when and how to do these things without conscious thought.

» Saying the right thing at the right time

» Being careful with fragile egos and sensitive temperaments

» Increasing the energy in the room just by showing up

» Active delegation and automatic involvement of the right people

» Intuitively balancing the needs of people while minding profit

As you go through the chapters of this book, you will find examples of skills and tactics that will be in all four categories of your competency ladder. Pay attention to where the recommended actions fall for you. This knowledge is crucial to you being able to best learn and leverage the new skills.

Recommendation: Share and teach these categories to other people. The competency levels will become more clear and distinct every time you discuss them with someone else or draw out an example using them.

The One Thing: _____

_____

Playbook Notes: _____

_____

_____

_____

_____

> "There are risks and costs to action. But they are far less than the long term costs of comfortable inaction"
> **-John F. Kennedy**

ORGANIZING YOUR PERSONAL BOARD OF DIRECTORS

THIS IS A VERY POWERFUL idea that we first introduced in Full Contact Leadership way back in 1996. We also had a segment dedicated to the tactic in What Exceptional Leaders Know. It has been the recommendation we get the most feedback about and the most success stories from. Because of that, we've decided to update and add more tactical recommendations to the Personal Board of Directors (PBOD) strategy here. We have added some detail and made the steps easier to follow. Let's get to it.

Everyone knows what a board of directors is. Most growth-oriented companies and start-ups organize a group of people with various talents and skill sets to help set the direction for the organization. Typically, the members are chosen because of a positive impact they can have on the decisions and strategies of the organization.

So how do we apply the idea of the PBOD to our personal development?

We all have smart people in our lives. People that know things we don't know. Using these relationships, we can leverage the power of the BOD to make sure we are constantly improving our skill sets and our awareness of areas where we can improve.

Norman Vincent Peale was the first to write about the power of this idea. He famously called it "The Mastermind Group" and wrote at length about using our relationships and our imaginations to drive purposeful self-improvement. He understood, as did his mentor Andrew Carnegie, the power of deliberate time being spent with people who can influence you for the better.

As ambitious people, we're going to be growing, learning, and changing throughout our careers. We shouldn't leave anything to chance, or rely on the "accidental influencers" we bump into. Being open to and deliberately in search of the right influencers will be a big part of reaching our potential as leaders.

SO HOW DO YOU START ORGANIZING YOUR PBOD?

Start by thinking about people who have positively influenced you in the past. Who are some of the people who have helped you have the success you have experienced so far? Keep your perspective open wide. These influencers will not just be people you worked with. Some of your most powerful influencers will be teachers, coaches, friends, authors, speakers, and peers. Think about yourself as you are right now. Then think about the professional you would like to be. Consider some of the exceptional people that you know who have some of the attributes you aspire to. With a little thought you will be able to identify (1) areas of your life where you have upside, and (2) someone in your life who may be able to help you in these areas.

Here are some prompts for areas where a board member may be able to have a positive influence. Keep your list of improvement areas pretty short; you can always add something new later. Your Board of Directors will be changing shape all of the time, to match up with areas of your life where you want to see change and improvement.

- » Financial
- » Life Balance
- » Nutrition
- » Parenting
- » Fitness & Energy
- » Technical Skills
- » Goal Setting
- » Being a Great Spouse or Partner
- » Improving your Hobby, Craft or Sport
- » Investing
- » Stress Management
- » Professional Skills

Now it is time to organize your personal Board of Directors.

Here are six key steps for putting your BOD together:

1. Think about yourself and your current performance. Ask yourself some simple questions:

What's working for me? _____

_____

_____

What's not? _

_____

_____

Who's influencing me now? _____

_____

_____

When do I have the most fun in my current role? _____

_____

_____

What have I been doing the same way for too long? _____

_____

_____

What are my greatest assets? _____

_____

_____

2. Think about some people who have some of the spirit,
   capability, attitude, enthusiasm, credibility, and influence that

you would like to have. They can be peers, friends, authors, speakers, bloggers, poets, musicians, celebrities, athletes… whoever. They can be dead or alive. They can be people you know or people you don't. Make a list of these people.

_____

_____

_____

_____

_____

_____

_____

_____

1. Review this list and think about what you would like to learn or assimilate from each person. Who on your list do you have access to? How will you access him? It can be in-person, over the phone, by reading her books, by seeing his work.

2. For the people you have personal access to, ask yourself a few more questions. Will this person give me some of their time? Will they give me unfiltered opinions? Can I do something in return? It's not necessary to tell anyone that they're going to be on your BOD, unless you think it will help the relationship.

3. Post your BOD somewhere you can see it and make a commitment to seek out input, content, lessons, and conversations in any form you can get it from the members of your board.

4. Review the concept occasionally and ask yourself if it's adding any value to your development. If not, you may need to be more active and overt, or you may need to shake up your BOD.

Why should corporations and start-ups be the only ones benefitting from an influential Board of Directors? Once your PBOD is in place, think about how your different board members may be able to influence your personal development.

It's a powerful idea, and once you see the impact of it, you can share it with other people you care about, including your sales team. I'll bet that you'll end up on a few boards of directors as well.

The One Thing: _____

_____

Playbook Notes: _____

_____

_____

_____

_____

COACHING
THE TEAM

> "Not finance. Not strategy. Not technology. It is teamwork that remains the ultimate competitive advantage... both because it is so powerful and so rare."
> **-Patrick Lencioni**

THE MATURITY CONTINUUM

THE MOST IMPACTFUL effort any leader can make on the results of an organization is to work on their own leadership skills and understandings. Most undeveloped leaders believe the exact opposite. They believe that it will be the work they do on others that will yield the best results. In fact, many would-be leaders think that this is the whole job of leadership, interventions, reassignments, evaluations, etc.

Progressive leaders know that everything starts with the coach. Over the last several chapters, we have outlined a series of strategies that will help any leader upgrade their leadership tool box. Now it's time to start working on the actions and strategies that will allow us to influence the performance of our people and organizations. Remember, exceptional leaders think about leadership as a verb. Leadership is a series of deliberate actions. It is something you do, not something you are.

As we begin to think about how our leadership can influence people and teams it is important to understand how organizations benefit from progressive leaders. Stephen Covey introduced the concept of the Maturity Continuum in his classic book The Seven Habits of Highly Effective People. The continuum is an excellent way to understand how high-performance organizations develop, and how leaders can influence that growth.

There are three stages on the maturity continuum, moving from dependence to independence to interdependence. These levels apply to people and to teams. For our purposes, we will apply the terms to organizations and describe how teams at different levels function. As you read through the descriptions you will know right away where your organization or team fits.

STAGE ONE: DEPENDENCE

This is a top-down organization. The leader takes care of the team. Final answers and decisions come from the leader. There is very little autonomy for team members and a tight chain of command. These organizations typically do not handle change well and people do everything they can to look good in the eyes of the leader, even if their reputations with their peers suffer because of it. This kind of organization or department does not develop other leaders. Loyalty is prized ahead of creativity or innovation. Often the leader of this kind of organization is the founder or owner.

STAGE TWO: INDEPENDENCE

The groups in this organization work independently. There is very little cross-pollination between groups. There is often a lot of cross-organizational blame when things don't go right. The leader tends to have a specific background and focuses on that area. People don't understand each other's responsibilities fully and the atmosphere can feel competitive even though each is necessary for the success of the organization. These organizations often develop through merger or acquisition. Often, the leader has been promoted over former peers.

STAGE THREE: INTERDEPENDENCE

This organization is in the "we" business. We can do it. We can meet the challenge or goal. We can do better. This kind of organization is always led by a developed leader. A leader who understands the power of recognition and delegation. A leader/coach who has realized that leadership is an action, not a position. The interdependent organization has unlimited growth potential because leaders are being constantly developed.

A DECLARATION OF INTERDEPENDENCE

This shift in perspective that is necessary for any of us to approach our full potential as leaders. It can be a difficult shift. It is a move away from ego, and it distances us from the authority of our title. It is another shift in the direction of humility. Leadership humility has been discussed in a few other places in this book, and it is popping up again here. There is no way to exaggerate the importance of humility in becoming an exceptional leader.

We all know that to be a truly effective leader we must truly value the people on our team. When we say, "truly value," we mean really understanding that they can do things you can't or won't do. On the human scale we are all equals, but on the organizational scale the leader will always have a broader span of responsibility, but the org chart is not the scale we are addressing here.

Truly valuing the people on your team means understanding that:

1. You are just as dependent on them as they are on you.
2. You will succeed or fail as a leader based on how well they do their jobs.
3. It is in your best interest as a leader that they understand and believe that their jobs are absolutely critical to the success of the enterprise.
4. The fact that one person has more responsibility than another does not make them more important.
5. Everyone depends on everyone else for the team to succeed

Number four above is the one that average leaders can't get their head around. They don't understand that it is their job as leaders to make sure everyone on their team is "mission critical". It is the leader who needs to make sure that their people know exactly how and why the success of the team depends on them.

Here's another secret exceptional leaders know: The lower the person is on the org chart, the more important the understanding of their "mission critical" status becomes. Managers and VP's know they are important, some of them will remind you constantly of their importance. Task workers and staffers are not so sure, and this gives you a chance to lead. Exceptional leaders know how to prioritize this kind of recognition and attention.

How do you eliminate this gap and move your team in the direction of trust and interdependence? Here is a short list of simple changes and ideas we recommend for closing the gap:

» Share problems and issues with your team. Don't be afraid of bad morale. Nothing is worse for morale than the collective sense that you are not sharing important information. Assume that they value their jobs and roles just as much as you do. Transparency is your ally in building trust.

» Keep your door open. Unless the conversation is absolutely private there is no reason for closed-door conversations in business. We are all here to succeed.

» Humility can mean a lot of things. Small acts mean a lot. Make the coffee, leave the best parking spot for someone else, and make sure someone's chair is comfortable, work in the common work areas. Don't always think your story is most important, don't one-up people under any circumstances. You are the leader. You get paid more. That is enough.

» Surprise people with involvement. Ask opinions about issues outside of their responsibility. It shows people that you don't always think you have the best answers. Guess what? You don't.

» Think about the ways you hold yourself above your team. Then think about the reasons why. The littlest habits can hurt you. For example, if it is your habit to always be a few minutes late to conference calls you are sending a message. The message is unmistakable. It is "my time is more important than yours". This is not an idea you want to be telegraphing to your team three times a week. Challenge yourself and make some changes where you can. They all count.

Acknowledging the interdependence of your team is one of the most powerful steps you can take as a leader. It requires a detachment from ego and the embracing of humility. It means relating to your staff as peers who just have different responsibilities to the organization.

This kind of democratic "team", free from the constraints of ego and position, will always outperform a traditional boss/subordinate arrangement. This acknowledgement of interdependence is at the heart of exceptional leadership.

The One Thing: _____

_____

Playbook Notes: _____

_____

_____

_____

_____

> "I think the currency of leadership is transparency. There are moments where you've got to share your soul and conscience with people and show them who you are"
>
> **-Howard Shultz**

THE POWER OF TRANSPARENCY

ONE OF THE MOST important character traits of today's high-performance leaders is transparency. We refer to it as a "character trait" because transparency, either the commitment to it, or the lack of it, is a reflection of the character of the leader. Historically leaders and managers have used a kind of calculated transparency to grow their own power. The decision to share or not to share certain kinds of information is one of the key differentiators between leaders and coaches.

Have you noticed that transparency is getting a lot of lip service these days? It has found its way into a lot of mission statements and corporate credos. The big question has become: Is transparency actually part of what we are doing as leaders, or, are we just talking about it?

To answer this question, we need to start with the basics. What is transparency? You will probably never find another strategy that is simpler to explain. In a team context, transparency means telling the truth to more people than you normally would. More staffers, more customers, more stakeholders, transparency means more truth to more people.

Transparency is aspirational; leaders and organization that value it will be constantly challenged with just how much transparency is actually good for their teams. We have worked with companies who deeply valued transparency as part of their corporate culture. They were overt in the discussion and debate of key strategic decisions. We have seen how this commitment to transparency has been very positive and absolutely negative in different situations.

The best way to show the power of transparency, and the risks of non-transparency, is through case studies. The following two studies reflect work with two of our corporate clients, and the stories are reported exactly as they happened. We have left the names of the leaders and organizations out to protect their privacy.

CASE STUDY #1 – ABC COMPANY

We worked with a company in the petrochemical industry that leveraged their commitment to transparency to great effect during a recent commodity-pricing crisis. The global value of their refined product had dropped so drastically that they were shutting down certain operations and initiating a staged furlough program for important workers in these locations. Their company was in the news and the experts in their industry were not certain they would even survive the pricing crisis.

We were in the room when the CEO addressed the team at their company headquarters. The leader had a reputation for his candor and transparency, even with bad news. He addressed the nervous executives with a calm demeanor, and explained the plans for what would have to happen if the prices continued to drop. Which personnel would have to be released and why, and what the company was trying to do to remain solvent through the crisis.

Next, he discussed how the company would ramp back up again once the pricing pressures were relieved and what that would mean for the people who had been let go. He understood what all great crisis leaders understand: the absence of information creates a vacuum, and what fills that vacuum is angst and fear. Presenting a tough truth, even when it is uncomfortable for everyone involved is almost always better that letting people's imaginations fill in the blanks.

In some organizations, the video does not match the audio. The leaders talk about the value of transparency and their commitment to it, but the team rarely sees it. This kind of false transparency does not engender trust or appreciation. Rather, the product of this lip service kind of transparency is cynicism and distrust. Unfortunately, many of the leaders who talk about transparency the most fall into this category.

CASE STUDY #2 – XYZ COMPANY

Let's look at a situation where transparency would have made a big difference. In this instance, the leader didn't think it was part of her job to make sure the team knew the situation they were in. The company was a mid-sized aerospace equipment company that had grown quickly to around fifty employees. Most of the fifty were fabricators in a large machine shop where the aluminum parts were milled and finished for shipment to their aerospace customers.

We were hired as consultants because the owner/president of the company was very concerned about the morale. She had reported that everyone was constantly in a bad mood, especially in the fabrication shop. Absenteeism and tardiness were way up and none of the good-natured camaraderie that had characterized the shop previously seemed to be there anymore, or at least when she was around. Business was slow but everyone was still getting paid, she said. She had even confessed that she and her husband (also on the payroll) had each gone without pay for the previous several months because the orders had dropped so dramatically.

We scheduled a series of one-on-one meetings with the employees. It was explained that their opinions would be considered confidential, so they could safely share their feelings. When we began the interviews we quickly found exactly what the owner had reported, these people were in a nasty mood. They had nothing but negative feedback on the business, the working conditions, the owner, the owner's husband; you name it. When we started asking for specifics we got a laundry list of slights and negative changes perpetrated by the owner. Here is the list:

» No more coffee service in the shop

» No more overtime pay for Saturday shifts

» No more free Friday lunches were being provided

» Two vending machines in the shop had been broken for months

» Shop employees were being asked to wash their own uniforms (no laundry service)

- » Company was no longer sponsoring the softball team
- » No holiday bonus was paid in December
- » And a few more general grievances

Now it was time to meet with the owner behind closed doors to review our findings. We were prepared to review the list and discuss how the accumulation of these complaints and grievances was affecting the overall morale and energy level of her business. We went through the entire list, being careful to reference when a particular complaint was mentioned more than once. We had asked the owner not to react to any individual items on the list; saying she should focus instead on the spirit of the complaints and how they might be affecting the working environment.

When we were done with the review the owner was silent for a while, and then she explained what was actually happening at her company. She said that one of her first priorities when she started the business was to provide stable employment for good people. In an industry with lots of ups and downs, she felt that being able to provide stable and consistent work would be a great way to attract and keep a great team, especially in the fabrication shop where the really skilled people worked.

She went on to say that every one of the comprises that had been made, the coffee, the lack of overtime on Saturday shafts, not repairing the vending machines, the unpaid holiday bonus, etc., were decisions she made to keep from having to lay anyone off. She added that she had not, in fact, laid a single person off during this entire down cycle in her business versus competitors that were aggressively laying people off.

We asked why she had never shared this information with the staff? Especially when the morale had gotten so low? She said that she did not want people to worry about their jobs or the company, because that was her job.

We scheduled a meeting the next day for all of the shop workers, the office staff, and the owner. We talked through what we had learned from both sides. The meeting ended with some tears, lots of hugs, and most importantly: understanding.

The bottom line was that this was a bad situation that could have been completely avoided with simple transparency. The workers did not trust that the owner was working in their best interest, and the owner had not believed that the workers could adequately grasp the business situation the company was in. Both sides were wrong.

A FINAL WORD ON TRANSPARENCY

Developed leaders and coaches understand that it is better to err on the side of too much transparency, rather than too little. When you offer too little transparency, you are risking your credibility. When a leader seems to be offering too much transparency, they open themselves to some criticism, but their credibility is not at risk.

Remember, transparency is just telling the truth to more people than you normally would. More staffers, more customers, more stakeholders; transparency means more truth to more people. It is a decision you are making about your organization's character. Making a habit of demonstrating real transparency in your role will make you a better leader.

The One Thing: _____

_____

Playbook Notes: _____

_____

_____

_____

_____

> "A coach is someone who tells you what you don't want to hear, who helps you see what you don't want to see… so you can be who you have always known you could be".
>
> **-Tom Landry**

COACH THEM UP OR COACH THEM OUT

WE TALK A LOT about how "leadership leaves clues" with our clients. What this means is that there is always clear evidence of exceptional leadership, or the lack of it, in any organization or department. We never have to guess about whether we are leading effectively, because our results are right in front of us every day. These results can show up in a lot of different ways. They can show up in the numbers, they can show up in your retention of talent, they can show up in your culture.

What is the clearest evidence of exceptional leadership? Here is what you should be looking for:

Improvement – People show tangible improvement over time

Capability – There is an understanding that everyone has upside, even you

Engagement – People are interested in other people's success

Bias for action – People initiate things, they don't just talk about what should happen

Expectation – The team expects everyone else to perform, it's what we do around here

<u>Coaching is leadership in action</u>. Think about how optimistic the act of coaching really is. Coaching someone means that you believe they can get better with some attention and expectation. It means that you know that they are full of potential and that you are eager to help them discover it.

In contrast, we meet with organizations all the time where people are clearly not improving. We find businesses and divisions where people are hired with a certain skill set which is basically their only long-term contribution to the team. They don't improve, because they're not expected to improve. This is typical of an organization without enough coaches.

We describe many coaching strategies throughout the book, but let's start with the most crucial understanding for leaders who are focused on improving their teams.

THE CRUCIAL DIFFERENCE BETWEEN CAN'T AND WON'T

This may be the most important distinction you ever learn as a leader. Leaders and managers who never learn to discern between "Can't" and "Won't" will have a career of frustration and confusion. We go so far in our training events to say that if this key distinction is all you know, you will still be more effective in your role than 90% of all leaders.

Understanding the seemingly simple difference between the two is the key to making good personnel decisions as a leader. Let's review with the definitions:

Can't – They don't know how to do it. It is a capability issue.

Won't – They refuse to do it, passively or actively. It is a motivational issue.

Leaders can create serious issues when they misdiagnose a situation and treat a Can't like a Won't... or vice versa. Here are the common mistakes:

Treating a Can't like a Won't – The leader dealing with a performance issue treats the team member like they don't want to perform. They make it more urgent. They involve other people. They express disappointment. This approach backfires because the person actually does want to perform, they just don't know how. There is a capability shortfall, it has nothing to do with their level of motivation or interest.

Treating a Won't like a Can't – The leader focuses on getting the person support, resources and/or training. They want to make sure the person can do the job. The problem is that the person doesn't want to do it at all, even if they know how. The lack of performance has everything to do with motivation, and nothing to do with capability.

Here are a couple of very typical examples of getting it wrong:

SCENARIO 1:

Performance Issue: Area sales manager refuses to let go of a dishonest person

Outcome: Initially the leader treated the issue as a Won't and pressured the manager... even doubting her loyalty to the company. The problem was that the manager had never released anyone and simply didn't know how to manage the conversation. She was delaying because she didn't know how to do it. Once the leader realized it was a Can't, he talked it though with the manager, role-played different responses, and expressed his confidence in her manager. She executed the conversation perfectly and now no longer fears this kind of situation. Coaching gave her new capability.

SCENARIO 2:

Performance Issue: Practice administrator is not organizing staff meetings

Outcome: Administrator was getting pressure from practice executives to start organizing weekly meetings. When nothing happened, the Administrator was sent to a leadership class on organizing and running effective meetings. Still nothing was scheduled and one of the executives did an example staff meeting with the Outlook invite, agenda, minutes, etc. just to make sure the Administrator understood what the executives were looking for. It was only after all of this that the Administrator finally said that he didn't think staff meetings were important and didn't want to start having them. They had treated a Won't like a Can't and gotten nowhere on the issue. Once they understood that it was a motivational issue on the part of the Administrator, the executives were able to address the issue accurately.

Think of a few performance issues you have had to deal with over your career. It can be very valuable to look at situations in retrospect… using the Can't / Won't question to consider what really happened.

Scenario 1 _____

_____

Can't / Won't

Scenario 2 _____

_____

Can't / Won't

Scenario 3 _____

_____

Can't / Won't

Here's a simple flow chart that shows the steps toward resolution of any performance issue. The first thing you have to get right is the Can't or Won't question. After that, things become pretty easy.

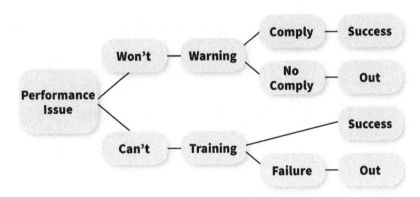

You will find that over time you will be almost automatically able to discern between these two very different kinds of performance issues. You will see much faster improvement and progress to positive resolutions. In organizations where we have trained the Can't / Won't paradigm the language even changes with the leaders. We'll hear them asking "is it a can't or a won't?" when trying to resolve performance issues. Adding this kind of discernment to your leadership skill-set is a difference maker.

The One Thing: _____

_____

Playbook Notes: _____

_____

_____

_____

> "The art of communication is the language of leadership"
>
> **-James Humes**

THE FOUR CONVERSATIONS YOU MUST GET RIGHT AS A LEADER

ALMOST ALL SUCCESSFUL leaders understand that effective leadership really comes down to influence: Influencing outcomes, influencing direction, influencing decisions, influencing atmosphere and influencing people. The degree that a leader can successfully influence people and teams becomes the "lid" in their role. The only reliable tool we have to influence others is communication. Any leader or manager who is serious about improving his own performance should always start with improving his communication skills and techniques.

Influential leaders are great communicators. They know what to say and when to say it, and they understand that effective communication is a study. It does not come naturally, and it needs to be worked on the same way a leader might work on his technical skills. We have all worked with would-be leaders who never seemed to get it right. They say the wrong thing at the wrong time. Or worse, they say nothing when something definitely needed to be said.

Your communication skills are your #1 leadership asset. This is especially true in high-performance environments or in organizations going through a lot of change. Leadership communication skills is a very broad topic. Today, let's focus on effective one-on-one techniques. We are going to review the four conversations we must get right as leaders.

CONVERSATION #1 - THE TIMELY TALK

This is a must-have conversation for specific situations. No leader looks forward to a Timely Talk because of the stress associated with it. How do you know it is time for a Timely Talk?

» Someone is underperforming and affecting the overall results

» Someone is creating issues for the team (any kind of issue)

» You are invested in them and they are not succeeding

» It is not going to improve without your intervention

Every situation is different, of course, but there are proven ways to have a Timely Talk. Most leaders will either avoid this dialog or go into it without any preparation. Top leaders know how to structure this talk for success.

Your Timely Talk Script:

1. Explain the reason for meeting (performance issue)
2. This (issue) concerns me because…
3. Make a clear coaching recommendation
4. Set up a review time and put it on both of your calendars
5. Clarify your confidence in the person

CONVERSATION #2 – THE ROCK STAR REMINDER

This one is so simple, yet very few leaders ever do it. Here's how you leverage this powerful communication tactic with a key person on your team:

» You have someone on your team with amazing potential
» They are still learning and improving
» They may be hitting some bumps in their career
» You expect them to do GREAT things
» You need to tell them!

This is the Rock Star Reminder. It is as important as it is simple.

CONVERSATION #3 – THE NOW OR NEVER CONVERSATION

Every skilled coach has had this kind of dialog, and none of them look forward to it. The leader needs to understand that the key to this conversation is timing. There is always stress and emotion involved, usually for both parties. If a leader has a "Now or Never" conversation too early it will feel like manipulation. If the dialog happens too late, there won't be enough time for the person to make the necessary changes. That is why the timing has to be absolutely perfect.

The Now or Never conversation should always follow a failed Timely Talk (#1). The person knows that the performance/behavior/issue cannot continue and has had some time to make changes. This person is now at risk.

The best way to prepare for a Now or Never conversation is with talking points. Lots of different things can happen in this dialog, so scripting your comments and questions is not the best way to prepare. Here are some effective talking points that will take the conversation where it needs to go:

- » "We seem to be stuck and we're running out of options"
- » "You are making a decision about your future with your performance, do you understand that?"
- » "Your potential in this role is as great as it ever was"
- » "I would hire you again if you walked in for an interview"
- » "This is the moment where things must change"

This dialog is the last chance a leader has to influence behavior. The Now or Never conversation is one that most leaders are unwilling to have. You can separate yourself from other leaders and managers with your candor and honesty.

CONVERSATION #4 – THE IVY INTERVIEW

IVY stands for I Value You. The IVY Interview is the conversation you have with a proven and valued team member who you very much want to stay. This important tactic is routinely overlooked, even in high-performing organizations. Do you want to surprise and impress your team with truly progressive leadership? Learn how to conduct the IVY Interview.

HOW DO YOU KNOW IT IS TIME FOR AN IVY INTERVIEW?

The recommended strategy is to add IVY interviews to your calendar, quarterly works best. Every quarter you will consider who on your team is really performing? Who might be being overlooked? Who is in a role that may have less recognition attached to it compared to other roles? Who seems to have a lot of upside? You are not really reacting to a certain accomplishment... you are paying close attention to sustained performance.

An important thing to remember is that you don't use the phrase "IVY Interview" with the candidate. That is an internal descriptor to help you remember what you are doing and why. As far as they are concerned you are scheduling a time for a conversation with them about their position and performance.

Another important detail is that you do not want to schedule a series of IVY Interviews. These are occasional and important one-off conversations. Doing too many or doing them too often will erase the positive effects.

HOW TO CONDUCT AN IVY INTERVIEW

The meeting should be set casually, and not as a part of a formal performance review. You would ask the person if they can set aside some time for you on a certain day. Make sure your tone is upbeat and positive, and don't set the time more than a day or two into the future. You don't want this valuable person worrying for a week about a pending conversation with the Boss.

When the day comes, keep things very casual. The only formal part of the meeting will be your preparation. Start things off by thanking the person for taking the time to meet. Next, tell them you have been consistently impressed by their performance. Be specific here, be certain to note the aspects of the team member's work that are excellent. For the people you are doing IVY Interviews with, this should be easy.

Tell them you want to ask them some questions about themselves and their job, and that you would appreciate candid responses. Your tone and body language will make it clear that they are in a safe environment with a leader that really values them.

GREAT QUESTIONS FOR YOUR IVY INTERVIEWS:

Here is a series of great questions for IVY Interviews. You will see a few that are very applicable to your situation and maybe a couple that are not. Add a few of your own questions to the list, maybe something specific to the mission or culture of your organization. Start of with general questions and then move to more specific topics.

» How are things going for you?

» Are you enjoying your work?

» What is the best part of your job?

» What is the part you enjoy least?

» If you could change something about your current responsibilities, what would it be?

» Do you ever have tasks that feel like a waste of time?

» Where do you see yourself in five years?

» Is there a task or process you do outside of your responsibility that you think we could improve on?

» Is there something that you think we may be focusing on too much?

» Do you see any growth opportunities that you think we may be missing?

» How do you feel about our working relationship?

» Do you have any coaching tips for me?

» Do you know how valuable you are to this organization?

These questions, along with the additional questions you add to the list, will guarantee a positive dialog with your team member. You will have opportunities to ask for more detail and possibly hear some great ideas, maybe even do a little brainstorming. The last question will give you an opportunity to tell the team member how much you appreciate them and their great work.

Your IVY Interviews should take around 20-40 minutes. Any shorter and it wasn't a substantive conversation. Any longer and you probably starting talking about other people or go off topic: 20-40 minutes is your sweet spot.

It would be hard to list all of the positive benefits of IVY Interviews. Many of the best outcomes will be invisible, but still powerful. You can strongly influence retention, culture, job satisfaction, expectations, working relationships, and much more. Adding the IVY Interview to your repertoire of leadership skills will put you in a small group of progressive leaders who know how to pay the right kind of attention to the right people.

Now you know the four conversations you must get right as a leader. Using these templates, along with your own thoughtful preparation, you will see your positive influence over people and outcomes grow exponentially.

Take a moment and think about how, and with whom, you should have these conversations. Remember, intention without action means nothing for a leader. Who should you be talking to?

Timely Talks: _____

_____

Rock Star Reminders: _____

_____

Now or Never Conversations: _____

_____

IVY Interviews: _____

_____

Here's a promise for you: these conversations will move your team and organization forward. The ability and willingness to engage with people is a fundamental trait of exceptional leadership. Communication skills are your #1 leverage point as a leader. We strongly recommend that you keep working on improving your skill set as a progressive and confident communicator.

The One Thing: _____

_____

Playbook Notes: _____

_____

_____

_____

_____

> "The medium is the message."
>
> **-Marshall McLuhan**

MARSHALL WAS RIGHT

MARSHALL MCLUHAN coined this phrase in his 1964 book, Understanding Media: The Extensions of Man. At the time he could not have known all of the ways today's leaders would have to excel at communication, or all of the media that would be available to them.

Today's reality is as simple as this: If you can't communicate effectively across several platforms you are not going to be an effective leader. If you aren't great at communication, you won't be a good leader, you won't be a good seller, you won't be a good coach, and you won't be an influencer.

Yesterday's professionals needed to be good at (1) in-person communication and (2) one-on-one telephone communication. Today's professionals have to master those two, plus (3) conference call communication, (4) webcam communication, and of course, (5) email communication.

Let's discuss some rules and tactics for these newer methods of communication. It is in your interest to be great at all of them.

CONFERENCE CALL COMMUNICATION

The conference call has become the de facto means of collaborative communication for business. Being great at conference call communication is not an option for a high-performance leader, it is a must. Here are some guidelines:

» If you are leading the call, thank everyone for attending and start with a summary agenda.

» Always start your calls on time. If you make a practice of waiting for everyone you are gradually training them that it is okay to be late.

» Never interrupt another person speaking on a conference call unless you have to. Interruptions run rampant on conference calls, it is the biggest reason why collaboration often fails on conference calls. If you interrupt, say "I am sorry... I talked right over you" and let the other person continue. Not only is this the polite thing to do, you will see that very quickly everyone else is doing it too.

» In a call where there is a strong difference of opinion or some contention among the participants, always be the quiet voice. The emotional person is the weakest person on a conference call.

» If the call is to collect feedback of some kind, always wait until last for your own input. It will allow you to consider everyone else's point of view and to think through your pertinent thoughts on the matter.

» Effective conference calls require pauses for non-extroverts to be able to contribute their thoughts and feedback.

» At the end of a call, always summarize and agree on the "to-do's" coming out of the call.

» Finish your conference calls on schedule.

WEBCAM MEETINGS

Webcam meetings are going to be the norm for most of us, if they are not already. Most of the conference rules above apply to multi-person web meetings as well. Here are a few others:

» Be mindful of your background. A distracting or unprofessional background will make it hard for you to hold people's attention by webcam.

» Make sure to optimize your camera angle before a webcam meeting. It should be at eye level or slightly higher. If you need to lift your laptop up on some books to accomplish this then do it. A webcam looking up at your neck or nostrils is not a good look.

» Test your audio before you start doing web meetings. Some Bluetooth and VoIP audio can be really poor. A wired microphone or headset is the way to go.

» Think about your lighting. Many people have lighting behind them during webcam meetings and it darkens their face. This makes it hard to see their facial expressions, which it the reason they are using a webcam in the first place.

EMAIL COMMUNICATION

We all know that email has replaced most of our phone calls, most of our memos, and all of our faxes. It was supposed to be a replacement for "snail mail" but has become much, much more than that. Being good at getting your point across in an email message will have a lot to do with your level of influence in your organization. It will absolutely affect your career. It is something you want to excel at. Here are some recommendations:

» Be very careful with "urgent" emails. The only way an urgent message is effective is if you almost never use it. Let's agree that we all get three exclamation points to use per year… and try not to use them all.

» Use a clean san-serif font for your emails. The best ones are Arial, Avenir, Helvetica, Calibri and Mircosoft sans serif.

» Be smart and compelling with your subject lines. Subject lines like "Let's have an argument" or "I was wrong" will guarantee your message being read. Other great ones: "Are you ready to get uncomfortable?", "What's in it for you?", "A short message on an important topic" and "Please read these 146 words". Most people don't bother to be creative, if you have an important message to send, it is worth your time to do it right.

» Spellcheck. Please.

» Use bullet points, they work much better than sentences and paragraphs.

» Always change the subject line when changing the subject.

» White space is your friend; add spaces between lines of text.

» Stay away from using graphical content in your signature if you can. It will often not translate through other people's networks and firewalls, just showing up as HTML code.

» Use black or dark blue colored text and a reasonably sized font.

» Try not to send email messages when you are emotional about the issue. Write the message and revisit it a few hours later or the next day. You will nearly always modify the message.

» Be careful with a built-in salutation. Using something like "Make it a Great Day" in your signature will not always be consistent with the tone of your message.

So there are your recommendations for conference calls, webcam meetings and email. Being a great communicator makes you an influencer. Be deliberate in your communication and don't leave it to chance. The medium is the message, and it is in all of our interest to master each of them.

The One Thing: _____

_____

Playbook Notes: _____

_____

_____

_____

_____

> "The first responsibility of a leader is to define reality. The last is to say thank you. In between, the leader is a servant".
>
> **-Max de Pree**

LEADING A NEW TEAM

IRST OF ALL, congratulations! Being asked to lead a new team is a fantastic opportunity for a leader. The situation allows you, possibly for the first time in a long time, to look at things with fresh eyes. Everyone gets a clean slate, the people on the team and the leader herself. It's a situation built for growth and meaningful improvement.

You will definitely want to do things in a way your predecessor did not. Fresh approaches, new ideas, new delegations, new ways of thinking about the business you're in, clear expectations; these will be key to your success with the new team.

This is one of those situations where your early moves will be very important and visible. You will want to have a plan.

PREPARING TO LEAD A NEW TEAM:

Step 1: Clear your mind of any current judgments, biases, and prejudices you already have about this new team. The biggest gift you can give your new team is a clean slate. This is true because the non-performers will get a fresh start and the performers will have to keep performing to impress you, the new leader.

Step 2: Make sure you understand the expectations for this transition. Why is the change being made? Why you? What do the stakeholders want to happen going forward? How will the success of this transition be judged? You need to know the answers to all of these questions before you can begin planning.

Step 3: Make sure that your previous team is being cared for. What will be happening to them? Is it in their best interest? Have you made sure you have publicized their successes adequately? Should someone on your former team be considered to take over for you? Have you said all of your "Thank You's"? Is there something you could do to make sure their transition is successful? Remember, it was your team that got you this new opportunity, not your boss.

THE BIG QUESTION: WHERE IS YOUR UPSIDE?

Here is what you need to identify, understand, and leverage during your transition. Every team has upside and opportunity, and the best growth opportunities are sometimes hidden. There will be obvious opportunities, but they may not be the best opportunities.

Here's what to look for:

» Raw talent

» Offices, departments, or divisions trending poorly

» Market opportunities

» People who may be in the wrong role

» 12-24 month trends. What's going up, what's going down… and why.

» Specialists

» People who know how to coach

» Small segments or departments that are trending positively

Some of these will become your priority areas for growth. This is your low-hanging fruit.

Now we move on to the challenging part of the transition, working with the team. Your early days will be a mix of confusing personalities and mixed motives. Everybody will be trying to figure out where their personal stock is with you. You will hear a dozen versions of "You know I am important, right?"

During these early stages the leader has to be in the questioning and listening business. You can start to set a tone by not being too impressed with anything that has been done in the past. With every interaction you will want to move from the rearview mirror to what is in front of you. Here are some example phrases to help you do this:

"That is amazing Karen, we are definitely going to need some of that problem solving energy going forward"

"That was clearly a big win Robert, it's exactly the kind of initiative and leadership that we will be expecting from everyone"

"That sounds like a really positive outcome Joe. Can you think through how that same approach might be leveraged going forward?"

SIX CRUCIAL QUESTIONS TO ANSWER ABOUT YOUR NEW TEAM

1. Who on your new team will be brand-new for you?

Is this a team you're familiar with, or are you going to be working with strangers? Brand-new people are a great opportunity for you. Your priorities, communications, and overall leadership style will be fresh with these people, and it will be easier to make an impact.

Brand New People: _____

_____

_____

_____

_____

_____

2. Who are the three to five people who will determine whether this transition succeeds?

Ignore titles, tenure, and previous performance. There will be a small group of individuals who will be the reason your new team succeeds or fails. It may not be immediately obvious to you who they are. You absolutely need to figure it out before you start making any big plans.

Crucial Players: _____

_____

_____

3. What are the targets we are trying to hit?

There are only two or three crucial measures for any department or business. It doesn't matter whether we're talking about a single department or a multinational corporation. There will always be just three or four metrics that will tell what is working and what is not. What are they for you? You will want to keep your mind on these targets as you think through how you will leverage your new team.

Key Targets: _____

_____

_____

4. What previous traditions or expectations should you eliminate?

These are the things that run on their own inertia. This is the "way we have always done it around here" stuff. It could be reports, meetings, routines or social expectations. Some of these things probably worked at one point, but have pooped out. Some of these things never worked. The easiest way to say that a forward view is more important than history is to cut these things out. Bonus outcome: you will find out quickly who the change-averse people on your team are.

Expectations/Traditions/Routines to Eliminate: _____

_____

_____

_____

_____

_____

5. Where are you going to get your growth or improvement?

This is the hardest part of the planning. There's the hidden upside in your new area of responsibility. Your predecessor couldn't see it, but it's there. The team members know where the growth opportunities are, so interviewing them will give you some instant clarity. Giving them a platform and asking their opinions will also help you earn "buy in" from your new team. After that, you will need to dig into the numbers and see what they tell you. Inevitably, your growth opportunities will surface.

Upside Opportunities: _____

_____

_____

_____

_____

_____

6. Where will you be firm and where will you be flexible?

This is a way of asking what's important to you. Every leader expects to have to show her teeth occasionally, but you have to pick your moments carefully. There will be a few no-compromise areas, but it can't be every area or you will lose leverage and credibility.

You want to look for great opportunities to demonstrate what's important to you… even if it makes people uncomfortable. Most of this you can accomplish with recognition, just by making a big deal of someone who is doing it the way you want it done going forward.

Firm: _____

_____

_____

Flexible: _____

_____

_____

FINAL RECOMMENDATION: GO WHERE THE RESPONSE IS.

This five-word recommendation can save you years of work if you really understand it. Leaders succeed and fail based on their ability to direct people's energy and attention. Team members will not always agree on that direction. When they don't, the leader will not get the energy and attention he needs to succeed in the project, the initiative, or the business.

So go where the response is: Pay attention to who is engaged and on board with what you're saying and doing. Trying to change people's minds can be a losing proposition; it puts too much attention on the areas that are not working. Instead, focus your energy on the people who get it. Make sure they're getting the attention, recognition, and resources to succeed. The others will catch on or they won't, but they will not be the deciding factor in the enterprise.

Being a leader in a takeover role can be a high-wire act. You must premeditate every move. You will be under scrutiny from above and below, so you need to make sure the decisions you are making are an accurate reflection of your priorities and values as a leader. You can leverage these recommendations to ensure your success in your new opportunity.

Surprise people with your high expectations, make sure they know they are going to be playing for a winning team.

The One Thing: _____

_____

Playbook Notes: _____

_____

_____

_____

_____

> "Accountability is the glue that ties the commitment to the result"
>
> **-Bob Proctor**

FINDING & FIXING ACCOUNTABILITY LEAKS

HIGH PERFORMANCE ORGANIZATIONS and teams depend on accountability. It's the fuel that great teams run on, and a lack of true accountability is almost always the reason why some organizations underperform.

Here's a definition of accountability we can probably all agree on:

Accountability = The obligation of an individual or organization to account for its activities, accept responsibility for performance, and to report results in a transparent manner.

Accountability leaks are those areas in an organization where accountability is missing… where no one really owns the outcomes. These leaks create serious risks for teams and businesses. Think of an area where your team has consistently underperformed. There's a very high probability you'll find an accountability leak right there.

Here are five great ways to identify and fix accountability leaks:

1. **Start with what's important**. Every organization, team or department has its own key measure of success. It could be sales, retention, revenue, feedback, EBITDA, customer service measures, recruiting, billed hours, clicks, etc. Make sure everyone knows what's being measured in their area of responsibility.

2. **Make results public**. Accountability leaks disappear with transparency. Leverage dashboards, flash reports, leaderboards, win sheets, etc. Everyone should know what measure they are responsible for and exactly what the results are.

3. **Make sure leadership is accountable to performance**. There's only one real measure of leadership, coaching and management effectiveness; the people on their teams improve over time. You might be surprised to hear that the executives and leaders in many companies are the accountability leaks. In a high performance organization accountability starts at the top.

4. **Leverage recognition as your multiplier**. Recognition of expected and exceptional performance is a key to sustaining accountability. Accountability doesn't just mean drawing attention to what's not working… it means making absolutely sure everyone knows where excellent results are coming from.

5. **Be on the lookout for "Teflon" people in your organization**. These are people that seem to operate without any accountability or ownership. They can be found anywhere on your org chart, and they make it a practice to

never have any poor outcome stick to them. Identify these people and make sure they know exactly what results they own.

Those are the top five ways to find and fix accountability leaks in your organization. Remember, wherever you have consistently poor results you probably have clear accountability leaks. Poor results and disappointing outcomes are symptoms of a lack of ownership.

Accountability in the workplace is to be cultivated, not enforced. Finding and fixing accountability leaks in your organization is the key to sustaining a high performance culture.

The One Thing: _____

_____

Playbook Notes: _____

_____

_____

_____

_____

> "If you get the culture right, most of the
> other stuff will take care of itself"
>
> **-Tony Hsieh**

RESETTING YOUR TEAM CULTURE

ARE YOU IN A COMPANY or division that has become so entrenched in metrics and profitability that your people may be wondering if they really matter? Do you need a reboot? Or to wipe the slate clean so you can erase the accumulated negative energy and begin again?

Of course, we all have to focus on the profitability of our companies so we can stay in business. Most companies are trying to figure out how to do more with less. In most organizations, everyone is busy putting out fires and no one is deliberately thinking about the employee experience. I'm not saying no one cares, I'm intimating that it's probably not obvious to the people at your company how much they matter.

There are tons of great stories of companies that have great work environments. Zappos, Quicken Loans, Salesforce, Intuit, CareerBuilder, Edward Jones, Alphabet (Google), Southwest Airlines, QuikTrip and many others come to mind. I'm guessing your company has been good at developing a great environment at times but can you sustain it? Has it been put on the back burner? Do you want to know how to bring back the fun? Or maybe even start having fun? Having your employees smiling and getting along with each other better?

Let's assume you believe you need to make a change. You want to do something about the employee experience. Where do you start?

You start with a face-to-face meeting and tell people they matter. You stop just talking about the company and you start talking about the people. You acknowledge that you want to make sure they know how important they are and you actually give your team permission to provide feedback. It is NOT you giving up control or changing directions in how the business runs, it's simply you listening to your biggest customer, the people that provide whatever goods or services your company provides.

Start with a small group or your trusted advisors or your direct reports. Tell them you want to excite the troops. You want to start an employee appreciation campaign. Or you want to reinforce the one you already have that's no longer effective. Nickname them the "Culture Club", or anything else you think is catchy!

THE LOGISTICS OF THE MEETING:

Get a giant post-it note pad and a bag of markers. Put your team into groups of 3 or more, depending on how many are in the room. Hand out one sheet and marker to each group. At the top of the sheet, write "employee appreciation". Have them brainstorm their ideas for employee appreciation. Give plenty of time to write down as many things as possible. Remember, this might be the first time they have thought of it.

Make sure they have a long list, so take whatever time is necessary. Next, have them select their top 3 ideas from the list. They will have to sell each other and come to consensus. After you have 3 top ideas from each group, bring them back together. Have each group present their top 3 to the rest of the groups. List all of the top 3's, then have the entire group debate and come up with a consensus top 3. Once they all agree on the top 3, then decide. Can you take on all 3 strategies at once? Or should you select one or two from the list to begin with?

Make a master list of every top 3 idea. Perhaps you can implement one or two each quarter. Also, this list is fluid. As the "Culture Club" comes up with more ideas, you can simply add them to your arsenal of potential changes.

Creating the list is the fun, easy part. Executing and continuing the program will require discipline and follow through. If this is not your strength, assign it out but stay involved. Perhaps you have a few people that belong to the "Culture Club". It's a group from all levels in the organization tasked with suggesting new ideas and keeping the ideas already generated moving forward. The group can be fluid. Select a few mainstays but allow some rotating members to keep fresh ideas coming in.

You might have to spend more time and money than you want but think of it as an investment. Having a group of dedicated, passionate people working at your organization will come back ten fold. If you have ever spent one dime trying to attract new customers/clients, remember your employees are the best advertising strategy you have.

Even if you never execute one thing on the list, giving people a voice can be the change that is needed. We're not advocating blowing smoke at people or just acting, we're saying if your budget won't allow some of these strategies to be implemented you can still make them feel valued by listening to their ideas.

What will surprise you most is how simple the things are on the lists that you will witness. It really takes so little to make people feel appreciated and valued.

Here are a few activities that we have seen of these lists:

» Pizza parties

» Bowling leagues

» Contests

» Flex time

» Suggestion Boxes

» Being "in the know" on upcoming changes

» Involvement in 'executive' decisions

» Coffee Service provided

» Movie tickets

» Dinner Gift Certificates

» Focus group participation

» Hand written thank you cards

» Birthday parties

» Trips

Paying attention to the perception of your employees will yield a better work atmosphere, more loyal employees, and more customers; which will all lead back to more profits. Remember, people can always go find another job but they can't always find another place where they feel like they matter.

The One Thing: _____

_____

Playbook Notes: _____

_____

_____

_____

_____

> "The easiest thing to do is react. The second easiest is to respond. The hardest thing to do is initiate."
>
> **-Seth Godin**

MAKING MEETINGS WORK

L EARNING HOW TO have successful group meetings, as a meeting leader and a participant, may be the single most impactful skill set you can develop in business today. Think about it, nearly everything that happens in your organization and in your career will happen as a result of meetings. Your ability to drive ideas, agendas and outcomes is of crucial importance if you want to get things done.

The ideas we review will apply to in-person meetings, conference calls, and web meetings. Let's start with something no one ever seems to talk about; the cost/benefit aspect of meetings, or "Meeting ROI".

THE MEETING AUDIT

Experts report that business people spend between 30-80% of their time in meetings, depending on the type of business they are in and their role in the organization. This time commitment has a lot of ramifications. Let's start by examining the expense of recurring meetings.

Here is a typical recurring meeting set-up: eight people meeting once a week for one hour to discuss projects and updates. That sounds harmless, right? Would you be surprised to learn that this one recurring meeting costs $20,000?

Here's the math: 8 people x $50 per hour (eight people average $100k salary with executive and staff attendees) x 50 weeks = $20,000 of un-budgeted, un-audited expense.

What if there are several of these kinds of meetings every week? What if we included the opportunity cost of people not producing, selling, servicing, creating, executing and developing during those hours. The expense would probably double.

<u>Bottom Line</u>: Meetings are very expensive; you will want to make sure you are doing them right.

WHY ARE WE HAVING THIS MEETING?

Meetings need to have a purpose. As we all know, many recurring business meetings run on their own momentum. Organizations have the "Monday staff meeting" or the "mid-week huddle" and they have been doing it for years. You just started a brand new year…. did you revisit your recurring meeting schedule and confirm the value and output of every recurring meeting? It would be a really good idea.

BEWARE OF THE E-MAIL "CC" LINE

Often we add people to meetings who are not central to the project or who will not have influence on the decisions being made in the meetings. Every single person invited to a meeting adds both cost and time to the meeting. Unless a person's feedback is crucial to the output of the meeting, they should not attend.

Additionally, extra people who are not central to the project are typically the same people who (1) take the conversations off topic, and (2) talk too much, in order to justify their involvement in the meeting.

WHAT KIND OF MEETING IS THIS?

There are eight basic types of meetings and it is important to know what you are trying to accomplish in every meeting you schedule. Some more ambitious meetings blend more than one purpose. Here are the eight basic meeting types:

» **Project Meeting** – Organized to keep an initiative moving forward

» **Decision Meeting** – The yield is a decision that the meeting participants agree on

» **Update Meeting** – Attendees from different departments share progress and news

» **Recognition Meeting** – Meeting to draw attention to people who are doing good work

» **Energizer Meeting** – Designed to amp up the collective energy around a project or team

» **Feedback Meeting** – Ideas are shared to get reactions & recommendations from a group

» **Alignment Meeting** – Organized to square people, projects and expectations

» **Brainstorm Meeting** – The desired output of this meeting is actionable ideas

It is very important to know what each meeting is about and how the event is going to move the organization forward. You really need to understand what a successful outcome of each meeting would be, and make sure all of the participants have the same understanding.

A great way to make sure you have a solid meeting objective is to simply be able to finish this sentence: "The meeting will be successful if we _____". If everyone in the meeting knows the end of that sentence you are far more likely to have a productive meeting.

MEETING HACKS: GREAT IDEAS FOR BETTER MEETINGS

Built-in Buffer & Recovery Time – This is a simple game-changing tactic for many organizations. You simply schedule your meetings to end before the top or bottom of the hour. Examples: 2:00-2:25 meeting, or 9:00-9:50 meeting

The Standing Meeting – A great way to shorten meetings and make them feel more action-oriented

Change of Venue – Have a recurring meeting somewhere else every once in a while

Make Them Shorter – Most meetings are too long. Try making your hour-long meetings 30-minutes meetings. 99% of the time it works just fine.

Switch the Leader – Ask someone else to run the meeting. They will bring a fresh perspective and new energy to the meeting.

Call them Huddles, not Meetings – Huddles imply action.... Break!

Invite a Customer, Patient or Client to Attend – A great way to add formality back to a meeting that has ceased to have importance.

Let's finish this section with the **Ten Commandments of Successful Meetings**. Following these ten rules will absolutely improve the efficiency and effectiveness of your meetings:

1. Invite the right people to the meeting
2. Set a clear agenda in advance of every meeting
3. Meeting leader arrives 5 minutes early
4. Try to go device-free in meetings
5. The parking lot for off-topic ideas is your friend
6. Keep meetings as short as possible
7. Attendees: Target 4-8 for live or 3-5 for conference calls
8. Preparation = The expectation of progress
9. Meetings always start & end on time... or early
10. Always conclude with takeaways & go-do's

Please leverage these recommendations to improve the purpose, focus and expected outcomes of your meetings, especially your recurring meetings.

We have seen a surprising disparity between exceptional leaders and average leaders in the area of meetings. We strongly recommend that you open up your calendar now and audit your meetings. Focus on recurring meetings. Are the right people invited? Are they the right length? Who should be leading them? Do you have an agenda? Should certain meetings be happening at all?

Remember: Better Meetings = Better Businesses

The One Thing: _____

_____

Playbook Notes: _____

_____

_____

_____

_____

> "Everything that irritates us about others can lead us to an understanding of ourselves."
>
> **-Carl Jung**

SUCCEEDING WITH DIFFICULT PERSONALITIES

YOU KNOW EXACTLY who we're talking about. The moment you read the title of this chapter, someone popped into your mind. As leaders we have to be able to engage and succeed with the gossips, the divas, the know-it-alls, the never-on-times, the brown-nosers, the grouches, etc.

In learning how to deal positively with difficult personalities, progressive leaders need to start with this simple question: What do they need from you and your organization that they aren't getting? What is the personal win for them? What truly is their core need? Is their difficulty because of them or is there a chance it's because of their circumstances with you? You can take a hundred different personality tests to figure out who YOU are, but self-awareness only tells you half of the story. It tells you nothing about the people you are responsible for.

We've done hundreds of keynote speeches, leadership trainings, management seminars, team-building workshops and here is one absolute truth: everyone loves to hear about themselves. We all love talking about ourselves and finding out that there is someone else in the world that sees things like we do. This is one of the many positive outcomes from group seminars and workshops. We discover that someone else organizes their closet by color and sleeve length, or someone else can't stand for people to be late, or someone that can't stand to be criticized, or someone else understands the need for a to-do list. There are a thousand other things that make us feel normal when we can see that someone else understands us.

Some people walk out of these seminars with an even stronger sense that they are normal or "right", and those people have missed the point entirely. The real point of all of the testing, seminars, workshops, books on leadership, etc. is first to create an understanding of who they are. Second, and more importantly, is to understand the needs of those we interact with on a daily basis. Knowing who you are and what you need is important, no doubt, but knowing who your team is and what they need is even more important to anyone responsible for leading a group of people.

What does it take? It starts with the research. There are numerous excellent resources out therefor for personality and temperament training. We suggest a few chapters in our last book "What Exceptional Leaders Know" as a good place to start. Chapters 31-38 focus on this important topic. But you don't have to read one single thing to begin the process of having a better relationship with the difficult personalities on your team.

Here are 4 simple strategies you can begin now.

1. **Don't react**. Pause the next time you are frustrated with them. Just ask yourself what do they need that they aren't getting right now?

2. **Don't make up a bigger story about what's really going on**. If we really don't like someone, the moment they rub us the wrong way we tend to focus on the entire story of why they are difficult to deal with. We unconsciously add it to the situation playing out in front of us and it enhances and exaggerates our reaction.

3. **Quit expecting people to change**. The biggest frustration we deal with comes from having unrealistic expectations of our people. Every time you are "surprised" by someone, ask yourself this: Is this a normal pattern of behavior? If it is, there's no need to be frustrated unnecessarily. You knew it was coming anyway, right?

4. **Tell them the truth**. This one is a biggie. We've counseled so many people dealing with difficult personalities that have never done the thing that is the easiest and fastest way to create change. Be honest. Just tell them how their behavior is affecting the team and the organization.

Yes, we said most will appreciate it. You won't be able to change everyone. Your job isn't to change them anyway, it's to make them aware of their behavior. Tell them the truth. Give them a chance to make the changes needed to be easier to work with. What do you have to lose other than a little bit of time and ton of frustration? We'll talk about how to have those conversations in another section of the book.

The One Thing: _____

_____

Playbook Notes: _____

_____

_____

_____

_____

> "I feel that a great coach is one that has a vision, sets a plan in place, has the right people in place to execute that plan and then accepts the responsibility if that plan is not carried out"
>
> **-Mike Singletary**

PROMOTING TOP PRODUCERS

THE BEST PLAYERS usually aren't the best coaches. Think about the golfer that has a natural swing, or the baseball player that gets a great jump on the ball, or maybe even the tennis player that has a 130 mile-per-hour serve. Is it nature or nurture? Let's agree that it's both. They had some ability and then worked their tails off to hone their skills.

How about you? Think about some of the areas where you have excelled in your life. How did it happen? You probably have examples where natural talent came through along with some skills that required plenty of training and practice. Now let's think about your career. How did you get promoted into the role you're in now? Were you a top producer at your company?

Most managers and leaders are promoted based on their individual level of performance and then asked to multiply themselves. That is, they are expected to know how to take what they know how to do, or what they understand and transmit it to others with the goal of improving a department or team.

Let's take a closer look at the high producer and what happens when you put them in a leadership role. This is how most promotions work, and there is a lot of risk in the process. The hardest part about coaching for a great player is relating to the inability of other people. In other words, a great player hasn't had to truly think about the basic mechanics of their sport after they have gotten proficient.

Back to the four stages of learning, it's our blueprint for learning new things. We know that any attempt to learn something new goes through these stages:

Stage 1- Unconscious Incompetence. You don't know what you don't know. It's actually a great state to be in. Oblivion. No awareness.

Stage 2- Conscious Incompetence. This is the worst stage of all. You now know that you don't know. You are fully aware that you are not good at something.

Stage 3- Conscious Competence. You know it and you can do it but you really have to think about it. It's mechanical.

Stage 4- Unconscious Competence. You know it and you can do it without even thinking. It's second nature.

Great players walk around mostly in Stage 4 of their chosen sport or profession. When you take that player and have them coach people that are in Stages 1, 2, or 3 and there will often be a disconnect. It's difficult to truly remember the details of stage 2 once you have passed it. Here's where great coaches are different; the great coach not only remembers the stage, but are also able to relate to the experience of the people that are working towards stage 4.

They teach them from where they are in the process of learning instead of expecting them to be in stage 4 right away. They have empathy along with the ability to provide step-by-step instructions to get the stage 4. They understand that the only way to get to stage 4 is awareness and practice.

So, what does this mean for leaders? The leader that can stay connected to the mind and experience of the employee/learner will be successful. The leader that just keeps expecting people to "be better" or "do better" will burn through people and not cultivate the potential of those they serve. You must be able to create a process by which your people can see exactly how they will succeed.

This is one of the fundamental downfalls of very talented people that are promoted. The inability to relate. If you are unconsciously competent and not able to connect to the conscious incompetence of your people, you will not be an effective coach or leader. They need four things from you to get to stage 4. They need a vision, a plan, repetition, and a cheerleader. Let's break these down one by one:

THE VISION.

This is simply crystalizing what they bring to the organization. It is not a mission statement or a daylong seminar, it's simply helping people see themselves as an integral part of the team. It's creating that picture of what it looks like when they are at their best. What difference can/will they make to the overall picture?

THE PLAN.

What exactly is needed for them to be really proficient in their position? Is it research? Training? Working with other employees? Studying? Talking to clients? Reading internal memos? Also, what *is* a reasonable time line for their learning curve? Make sure they understand expectations.

REPETITION.

Let's add feedback as well. Practice doesn't make perfect, it makes permanent. If you don't meet regularly with your developing people and give them feedback, they'll just get better at doing it wrong. A coach must provide constructive criticism and positive expectations to move people the stage 4.

LASTLY, YOU MUST BE A CHEERLEADER.

What? You didn't sign up to be a cheerleader? What is you don't have the time or the patience to get people up to speed? Then you have two options: (1) Surround yourself with very competent people that can serve as a buffer and help you, or (2) continue to lose great people to other opportunities. This might seem harsh but the most important job of a leader is to develop other people.

The performance of the team is the most accurate reflection of your coaching. Spending time helping other people grow in their position is the true job description of leadership. The payoff? A high-performance culture with infinite possibilities.

Here are a few questions to consider from a coaching perspective:

Who do you need to pay more attention to?_____

_____

_____

Who comes to mind when you think about someone not living up to the potential you saw in them when they were hired?

_____

_____

What is your role in their current trajectory? _____

_____

_____

Who on your team needs to know that you see greatness in them?_____

_____

_____

Perhaps you have a few calls to make. I know we do.

The One Thing: _____

_____

Playbook Notes: _____

_____

_____

_____

_____

> "The growth and development of people
> is the highest calling of leadership"
> **-Harvey S. Firestone**

MACROMANAGEMENT & THE MAGIC QUESTION FOR MANAGERS

THIS TOPIC IS MEANT for front-line managers. These are the hard-working leaders who have direct influence on the work being done in any organization. This is the leadership segment where the real day-to-day coaching takes place. These managers succeed or fail based on their ability to positively influence their teams.

Unlike top-tier executive leaders, these leaders will actually be directly responsible for what their people do, and how good they are at it. They are the branch managers, sales managers, floor supervisors, department heads, store managers, etc. There is no room for theory or conceptual thinking here, there is too much to do. The front-line leader has a powerful and very responsible role. If this is you, pay close attention to what we are going to cover in this chapter, it can make your life a lot easier.

Daily life for a front-line leader is full of interactions and interventions. These interactions are with the people both above and below you on the org chart. They are your customers, clients and peers. These interactions are mostly daily routines. They are the connecting points for you and your teamand they usually don't require much thought or strategy. Interactions are what keep you busy.

All of these interventions are completely different from one another. Interventions happen when things are going wrong. Interventions are conscious interruptions in the momentum of your business. They happen when the status quo for a person or a process is just not working.

Interactions are part of the flow of your work. They are mostly automatic and don't require much forethought or planning. No so with interventions. They are never automatic, and a leader is never quite sure when one is needed. Interventions happen for a lot of reasons:

>> Someone is not doing the job
>> People are not getting along
>> Someone is becoming a distraction
>> Someone is not following the rules
>> Someone is putting a customer or client relationship at risk
>> Someone is forming bad work habits

These are all situations that require management from you. The situation is not going to fix itself and the leader has to decide exactly what needs to be done and when. These are always the two variables that define an intervention… what needs to be done and when. It sounds pretty simple, doesn't it? Every successful manager in the world knows that these decisions are not simple at all.

We've all worked with ultra-interventive leaders and managers who jump into every situation they can as if that really was the job of a leader. Some of these managers believe that that is what leadership is, attacking the situation, intervening every time anything is not being done exactly right. They don't even know there is a leadership decision involved with these actions. It is these constant interventions that defines the micromanager or helicopter manager, buzzing around getting involved in everything.

When it comes to interventions, we all have a leadership bias. Some of us are very involved managers, eager to intervene and try to quickly fix whatever is broken. The rest of us are more patient and hopeful that situations can resolve themselves. There are management challenges being in either group, and no one gets it right every time.

Here is where the Magic Question becomes so important and useful. It will help you make good intervention decisions, regardless of whether your bias is to intervene quickly, or to bide your time and hope the issue resolves itself. You will see that it is connected to the maturity continuum we reviewed a few sections previously.

The Magic Question for Managers:

"<u>Will this intervention create more independence or more dependence?</u>"

That's it. You should have a conversation with yourself and really think about what the result will be. "If the intervention is successful, and I (as the leader) have changed some behavior by getting personally involved, have I created more dependence on me, or some additional independence for the people on my team?"

This is the magic question because an honest answer will help you make the right decision most of the time (remember, no leader gets it right every time). We all know that managers and leaders who continue to build up dependencies with the people on their teams have a very low performance lid. Their teams cannot become truly high-performance teams because of their over-dependence on the leader. We've all seen how overly-interventive leaders can stunt the growth of their people.

Micromanaging is a habit with two really negative outcomes. The first is it will negatively impact the confidence and independence of your team, as we have discussed. The second negative outcome is that micromanagement is always one of the most hated attributes of managers on employment surveys. Worse yet, the people who like it the least are your best and most capable workers. Micromanaging can be a real retention risk.

If you are a recovering micromanager there are things you can do to get better fast. Start with the Magic Question to help you make good decisions about when to get involved in a situation. Another key part of improving in this area is to understand where the tendency comes from.

Geoffrey James published a great article on Inc.com entitled "5 Traits of a Micromanager and How to Fix Them". Here is his summary of the traits found in micromanagers and his recommended solutions:

1. MEASURING TOO MANY THINGS.

The advantage of technology is that you can measure your business more accurately. The disadvantage is that technology makes it too easy to measure too much. Measuring so much that it's not clear what the data really means is classic micromanagement.

What to do instead: For every job, select one or two metrics that define success for that job. Ignore everything else.

2. MONITORING TOO CLOSELY.

Monitoring is sometimes confused with measurement, but the two are different. You measure data; you monitor behavior. Monitoring becomes micromanagement if you're always looking over employees' shoulders.

What to do instead: Let employees request monitoring and coaching if and when they feel the need to improve their performance.

3. BUILDING TOO MUCH CONSENSUS.

Gathering inputs before making a decision is a good idea, especially from the people who'll be affected by the decision. However, you're micromanaging if you end up discussing things to death before making a decision.

What to do instead: Set a deadline for the decision. Schedule a limited amount of meeting time to gather inputs. Then make the decision by the deadline.

4. INTERVENING TOO MUCH.

Helicopter managers are as bad as helicopter parents--they create helplessness in the people they're trying to help. The only way that people can grow is by making mistakes, which means that the manager can't jump in all the time to fix things.

What to do instead: Provide guidance when asked, but let your employees fail. If they can't or don't learn from their mistakes, they're not worth keeping as employees.

5. SETTING TOO MANY PRIORITIES.

Managers confuse employees (and themselves as well) when they have a list of "priorities" all of which are more or less equally important. This creates micromanagement because that's the only way to "keep all the plates spinning."

What to do instead: Set one overriding priority for each employee, each team, each group and each division. Let them sort out how to achieve that goal or objective.

Geoffrey James – Inc.com – 5/2014

MACROMANAGEMENT

"Macromanagement" is a great word to describe how the most progressive and successful leaders choose their level of involvement in the day-to-day running of their business or department. They make their involvement and intervention decision based on the big picture of what they are trying to do with their teams. They have macro questions in mind like:

- » What are we trying to become as a team?
- » How am I building more capability?
- » How do I discover hidden upside on my team?
- » Who are my specialists and experts?
- » How can I help my team develop more autonomy?

Exceptional leaders are in the confidence business. They leverage everything they can to build up the confidence and expectations of their team members. People on their teams develop and succeed because they are not afraid to make mistakes or to do the wrong thing. They know the leader has more experience than they do. They also intrinsically know that a lack of heavy hands means that the leader believes in them and their abilities.

Great teams are characterized by individual responsibility and autonomy. Mistakes get made, to be sure, but these mistakes are also the learning opportunities and teachable moments that help people grow professionally. Leaders who can learn to be patient, and only intervene when they must, develop much more independent teams and a correspondingly higher performance lid.

In the days ahead, try not to automatically decide to intervene in a performance situation. Really consider what you are trying to build, and ask yourself the Magic Question. Over time you will become much more discerning and see the ultimate payoff; a more independent and confident team.

The One Thing: _____

_____

Playbook Notes: _____

_____

_____

_____

_____

> "Everyone rises to their own level of incompetence"
>
> **-Lawrence J. Peter**

APPLYING THE PETER PRINCIPLE TEST

L ET'S START WITH some background on the Peter Principle itself. The idea was presented by authors Dr. Laurence J. Peter and Raymond Hall in their 1969 book The Peter Principle: Why Things Always Go Wrong. The principle is that, in hierarchical organizations, people get promoted up to their level of incompetence, and stay there.

That means that over time nearly everyone in the organization ends up in a role where they are not performing at a high level, or in a position where they are incompetent. The book was written in the tone of serious business research, but it was actually intended as satire. The examples used in the book are fabrications.

That didn't matter at all because the principle resonated with business people and managers who could see how it could absolutely be true. People do a good job and get promoted. It is only when they are not doing a good job that they fail to be promoted. So that is the role they stay in, often for a very long time. Eventually a company is full of people who are not good at their jobs. The book was a New York Times bestseller, and is still in print after almost 50 years, so they must have gotten something right.

Could your organization be an example of The Peter Principle? There are some ways to find out. Think through these seven questions, and apply them to your situation. We will add comments about how PP (Peter Principle) organizations do things.

THE PETER PRINCIPLE TEST

1. **Does your organization apply and measure objective performance at all levels, or just for lower and mid-level people?** PP organizations are much more likely to objectively measure performance at lower levels, and use subjective measures and impressions for higher-level people.

2. **Does the average tenure of your employees rise from the bottom to the top of your org chart?** PP organizations are always stacked at the top with very long term people who rose into their roles over many years. Non-PP organizations tend to have tenured people all over the org chart.

3. **Do both regular employees and leadership have roughly the same percentage of their compensation tied to incentive targets?** PP businesses limit the incentive

compensation as people move up in the organization. They are paid just to be in their role, not to perform in it.

4. **Where is your professional development budget targeted; on entry-level, mid-level, or upper-level people?** PP organizations tend to think of professional development as something for lower and mid-level people. High performance organizations expect everyone to keep getting better at what they do, especially leaders.

5. **How long has the average manager in your organization been in their current role?** PP businesses always seem to have managers in roles forever, eschewing cross-training and reassignments.

6. **Are promotions in your organization based on objective reasoning? Is the performance you are rewarding with promotion clearly measurable?** PP businesses promote on seniority and loyalty, rather than performance and demonstrated upside.

7. **What percentage of your managers and leaders were promoted organically from within your organization?** PP organizations are far less likely to import leadership from other places. This "organizational nepotism" is a way of cementing the status quo and keeping disruptive people out of the company.

After applying these questions to your organization you'll have a good idea if your team may be at risk of being in a Peter Principle organization. Many of the tactics we discuss in this playbook can and will overcome this risk, but seeing things for what they are is step one.

The One Thing: _____

_____

Playbook Notes: _____

_____

_____

_____

_____

> "Train people well enough that they can leave. Treat them well enough that they don't want to"
> **-Richard Branson**

RECOGNITION IS THE MULTIPLIER

MANY PROGRESSIVE BOOKS on leadership correctly identify *positive recognition* as one of the most powerful means a leader has to influence results. Leaders who take the time to recognize where success is happening on their teams will always out-produce leaders who focus on what is broken or what's not working with their teams. This is Leadership 101, yet many would-be leaders just don't get it. Often, that is because they themselves have never had an opportunity to work with a leader who had learned the necessary sensitivity and skills to lead positively.

Many underachieving managers think of positive recognition as a soft skill of sorts. They think it is something that serious business leaders and high-level executives can leave to someone else. Of course, they are wrong. Exceptional leaders know how to influence people and action with recognition.

They know that positive attention being paid to success is the best way to: (1) make sure their successful people know they are valued; (2) make sure that whatever is succeeding continues; and, (3) clearly and strongly influence the behavior of the people who are not succeeding.

As most accomplished leaders know, the ability to recognize success and catch people doing it right is at the forefront of all leadership attributes. It is central to the desire to positively reinforce actions that we, as leaders, want to see repeated by the people on our teams. Unenlightened or under-skilled leaders tend to focus on the things that their team members don't know and the actions they are not taking, thus reinforcing these failing images in the minds of the people they are paid to help.

While it is important to be able to provide constructive comments, it must be balanced with positive recognition. Any leader can become great at identifying and recognizing the many little actions and decisions that lead to long- term success. They will eventually see the team consistently develop as the leader builds positive, reinforcing, relationships with them.

Let's discuss what kinds of things we must pay attention to as we help our team build their self-images as improving and succeeding professionals on a high performance team. It is our job to look for what we have come to call "Success Events". These are the many little and big things that happen along the way when someone is learning to succeed in a particular role.

These events break down into three general categories: (1) Performance Events; (2) Demonstrations of Effort; and, (3) Exhibitions of Attitude and Commitment.

We will list a few "Success Events" for each type. Together, we can get better at seeing these events when they happen and be able to recognize them properly.

PERFORMANCE EVENTS

This is the easiest area to pay attention to because this category focuses on results. Every kind of successful result can and should be recognized. Results like sales, customer service victories, documented improvements, client commendations, hitting or exceeding desired targets, cost savings, promotions, landmarks, and every other kind of positive result. Most companies make an effort to recognize performance, they just don't take it far enough. Usually firms only recognize efforts that have direct affect on revenue or customer satisfaction. Keep in mind, there are specialists and role-players all over your organizations who do a great job every day and would be sorely missed if they were no longer part of the team, even if they are in a low-profile job.

Does your office have a receptionist who is never late? You would certainly notice if he was constantly late. So how about some recognition for reliability? Does your website function perfectly? Someone is responsible for that. Does your mailroom run like clockwork? Who's responsible for that excellence? How about payroll or HR? Paying attention to solid performance is never a mistake. Look for it on all levels, and do not let people fade into the background just because they have been on the team for a long time, doing their job.

EFFORT EVENTS

This is the "cause" part of the cause-and-effect equation in any organization. As leaders, we need to be especially diligent to the attention we pay to efforts that we know will lead to meaningful results. The results are usually obvious to everyone, so being finely tuned to the efforts our team members are making is a key leadership element.

An important sale, a key improvement, or an exceptional customer interaction is always the result of some unique effort made by a committed individual. It is especially important to recognize quality effort when the result is not clear to everyone. Often teams do not accurately connect the effort and the eventual result. Other good examples of sincere effort are participation in office work, team members working on themselves through seminars or continuing education, staying late or arriving early, or aiding someone outside their department. Anything above and beyond a person's norm can and should be acknowledged. Intelligent effort or an "above-and-beyond" contribution should never go unrecognized.

ATTITUDE & COMMITMENT EVENTS

These are the events and actions that convey a person's belief in themselves and their commitment to the team. These actions are not always overt or obvious. Leaders must have their antenna finely tuned to catch these kinds of recognition opportunities. They are easy to miss and yet they are very important. Some good examples of attitude and commitment events are: taking responsibility for something outside of your department; a very enthusiastic interaction with a client; someone talking to the right influences; written goals; heavy involvement in a meeting; encouraging a friend or relative to apply for a job in your organization; offering up creative ideas; attending a seminar or meeting that requires an investment of time or money; and many, many others.

Providing a place where people learn to be excellent means that we must all learn the art of recognition. Here is a timeless (and unbreakable) rule of management: <u>what gets rewarded gets</u>

<u>repeated</u>. If that were the only leadership idea you knew, you could succeed as a leader and team developer. Many aspiring leaders do not succeed because they never grasp this rule. Don't let that be you. It is interesting to note that the phrases we all use to describe these positive actions sound like they are actually describing some kind of financial compensation: "paying" attention; "spending" time; "rewarding" with recognition. This is no accident. Recognition is an important part of how we compensate people for their efforts at work. Many studies over the years have shown that most people rate positive recognition as more important than financial compensation when discussing job satisfaction.

Those of us who forget to pay positive attention to our people or "can't find anything good to say" are, in fact, saying plenty. There are great things going on in your organization. If there's not, then it's your job as the leader to create headlines yourself. Make "paying attention" the number one item on your job description.

The One Thing: _____

_____

Playbook Notes: _____

_____

_____

_____

> "Leadership is the capacity to translate vision into reality".
> **-Warren Bennis**

A COACHING BLUEPRINT

ONE OF THE THINGS we have enjoyed most through our consulting is all of the time we get to spend in different team environments. We like to go where the positive action is, where there is a thriving business that is interested in further developing its people. We also see desperate organizations trying to make deposits with people where it is clear that too much has already been withdrawn.

Every organization and team is different, and it's always interesting to see the contrasts between them. The most striking aspect about successful organizations is their relative similarity. In other words, what works in one place usually works in another. Successful organizations all seem to operate on a similar frequency, regardless of the type of business they are in. We think that this is the vibration that occurs when a truly capable leader leads an organization; it just feels right.

The opposite is true too. An office or organization that does not perform seems to have a certain personality too. We've become so sensitive to these vibrations (for lack of a more descriptive word) that it's almost come to the point where we believe we can tell you whether a certain office or operation is a successful one just by the feel of it, without even meeting any of the people in the organization or seeing any kind of results.

Over our travels and many meetings with business people all over the map, we have come to a few key realizations that have formed the cornerstones of the Exceptional Leaders Lab's philosophy.

A. The leader must trust that intelligent effort from people is always going to be rewarded. When good people with good intentions do their best at something, it is always going to succeed. It may be sooner or it may be later, but success is on its way.

B. The leader will gradually develop an unshakable confidence in their ability to create an atmosphere that compels performance. Over time, top leaders are able to create a place where people will expect to be excellent at what they do. That place can be an office, a department, a division or a whole company. Leaders are thermostats, not thermometers.

C. The exceptional leader has an unwavering faith in the power of the individual. What we mean by this is that success or failure will always come down to a personal decision. Even in the worst of circumstances there are people who will succeed. You will also find people who have been given every possible advantage yet still fail to even approach their real potential. The essence of the individual transcends leadership and circumstance.

What a leader can do is provide a place where excellence can happen. The leader can create momentum and provide a positive example of success. The leader can set a compelling expectation of results and performance. Even with all of this, the ultimate decision about performance and success lies with the individual.

SUCCESS & FAILURE ATTRIBUTES IN PEOPLE

We've organized a list of five critical attributes we have seen demonstrated and repeated among the top achievers and leaders that we have worked with over many years. These are the traits that recur consistently in people that succeed. These are the traits that leaders should look for when building or adding to their teams.

We strongly recommend that you review these and consider them, as we have. Following that list, we have included another five-item list of some characteristics we have found that severely limit people. These are some of the attributes that will very likely make a person a liability on your team. You have seen them all before, but they are worth reviewing.

Here are some of the attributes shared among the top performers we have had the opportunity to know and learn from. You know the kinds of people we are talking about—those people who constantly transcend their positions to influence the rest of us. The performers who can always focus, can always "will" the proper outcome and who always seem to land on their feet. These people make up a critical minority in any company, and we all benefit from their effort and example.

It's important to have role models in any organization. They help the rest of us to see ourselves crashing through the same walls and leaping the same tall buildings. Businesses need heroes too.

THE FIVE ATTRIBUTES OF TOP PERFORMERS:

1. <u>They are results oriented</u>. They consider performance a part of their personality. These people are infatuated with what works. Most top achievers spend a little time discovering what will allow them to succeed and lots of time doing those things, rather than the other way around. They love how reliable the fundamentals are in business. They love being surrounded by other people who know how to make success easy by paying attention to what works. They want to be recognized as reliable performers and respond positively to challenges.

2. <u>They are tough</u>. For some reason, "toughness" does not get mentioned much when success characteristics are discussed. Make no mistake; achievers are tough as nails. Top performers must work through and around their circumstances. Their lives have the same challenges as anybody else's; they are just driven more by their mission than by their mood. One of the things from which I benefited when I started in business was a total lack of self-deception. My manager went out of his way to explain that success in business (and especially in direct sales where I started) is not easy and certainly not for the weak of resolve. He was right.

3. <u>They have a long time perspective</u>. Top performers do not judge their success or failure with short-term measurements. Short-term metrics are just not reliable for making important decisions or key adjustments. They know that they can become very successful by becoming truly excellent at a few disciplines. The great news is that the disciplines they

must learn to be successful in a business environment are the very same disciplines (goal setting, ethical behavior, active listening, mental toughness, continuous self-improvement, hard work, results orientation, etc.) that will help them in all the other aspects of their lives as well.

4. <u>They have an entrepreneurial approach to their work</u>. They are in business for themselves, but not by themselves. They really are their own brand. They realize that, in order to have a positive impact on their organizations, they must often be able to motivate themselves and operate independent of others. Top performers are essentially running their own personal service corporations. Most very successful people have this kind of entrepreneurial mindset even if they are not actually entrepreneurs. They know what they want to be known for and strive to live up to their own unique expectations.

5. <u>They have decided to make a difference through their work</u>. They put a heavy value on their personal brand. They don't just work through the week to get to the weekend. These people clearly feel they have a mission (regardless of their position) and understand where their individual success fits into the company's overall success. Representing a quality organization and doing quality work gives them a wonderful opportunity to serve.

Now let's consider the other half—those who can't seem to make things happen. The people who never seem to make any meaningful progress in their careers, and consequently, can be real liabilities in their organizations. If we were all paid on the basis of good intentions, these people would be millionaires. They are the

"80" part of the 80/20 rule. We have come up with what we think are the five major reasons people don't reach their potential at their work. You will find people who have these negative attributes at all levels of organizations. See if you recognize any of them.

THE FIVE COMMON ATTRIBUTES IN UNDERACHIEVERS

1. <u>People who fall in love with their limits instead of their possibilities</u>. It is easy to be seduced by excuses. Why? Because we all have them. Are mine better than yours? Are hers better than his? It is possible to spend a lot of time thinking about these things. Many people are far more comfortable with the surrender than they are with the work. Deciding to focus on your perceived limits is a choice, just like pursuing goals or improvements is a choice.

2. <u>People are often much more aware of what they don't want to be than what they do want to be</u>. We are constantly hearing people describe (in impressive detail) exactly who and what they don't want to be. They say they could never be really ambitious, or self-serving, or money-motivated, dictatorial or a workaholic. We always wonder how incredible these folks could be if they had spent as much time figuring out what they actually would like to become.

3. <u>Forgetting to work on themselves</u>. This is a big one, and it is discussed throughout this book. To succeed in the fast-paced world we live in now (and enjoy it), we must work on ourselves as hard as we work on our jobs. Incredibly, the act of self-improvement is also your best career move. To be the same as you were five years ago with no new insights, skills, philosophies, or lessons would be the saddest of outcomes.

It should be seen as an embarrassment not to be developing. We all seem to have time for lunch, small talk, television, gossip, why can't we find time to read or think?

4. <u>They look for short cuts.</u> For many people the apparently shorter, riskier route is much more attractive than the longer reliable one. We are often stunned by the lengths to which otherwise normal people will go to avoid simple and necessary work. This is another trait you will find as often at the executive level as anywhere else. There are people who will invite all kinds of career risk into their lives just to avoid doing some part of what they are paid to do.

5. <u>People who never really decide why they come to work in the first place.</u> All developed leaders understand that the "why" part of success will always overwhelm the "how" part. It's true. The functions are easy in most job roles. Interestingly, the functions of many careers have barely changed in the last 100 years. The tools have changed drastically and will continue to do so. But you can read a book on success written in 1940, and it will still have great (and currently applicable) advice. Why are they here? What meaningful things are they working toward? If they don't know, then the work they are doing will be sub-par and will not improve. Individual performance needs a context.

The two lists above are for generalizing purposes only. We would expect that you would add these learnings to your own personal lists. Developed leaders are constantly considering their experiences with different types of people. This allows them to, over time, accumulate a very valuable sense of who can succeed on their teams. These accumulated people-learnings can be priceless. They allow a leader to put together a high performance team very quickly, or to fix a broken team fast. An exceptional leader will become known over time primarily as an excellent team builder. Understanding people and what drives them is a necessary study for any serious student of leadership.

The One Thing: _____

_____

Playbook Notes: _____

_____

_____

_____

_____

> "A leader's attitude is caught by his or her followers much more quickly than his or her actions"
>
> **-John Maxwell**

LEADERSHIP & TIME PERSPECTIVE

L EADERSHIP TIME PERSPECTIVE can be described as the ability of the leader to be in the moment, even while they are thinking forward. Exceptional leaders can see what is and what can be at the same time. They react to events in the present with the future in mind. They understand how their directions and interventions can succeed in the present and borrow from the future.

Every leader has a natural time perspective setting. It is a function of their role, their personality and their responsibilities. This setting is the length of time they are usually considering when they make leadership decisions. Leaders are incredibly different from one another when it comes to this setting. Some front-line managers are set to succeed through a day or week. Middle managers are usually locked in on the month or quarter. High level and executive leaders must necessarily have a longer view. They should be thinking about years and decades.

Something interesting happens when managers and leaders

have a time-perspective setting that is not normally consistent with their role. When a lower level leader begins to think about a longer period of time in his decisions, moving from the week to the month or quarter for example, the consequence and outcomes of daily decisions come into view. This manager might start making completely different and better decisions about people, tactics and team development.

Consider another situation: An executive starts making decisions with a shorter and shorter period of time in mind. The executive might move from the long view with people development and brand equity in mind to short-term targets. Very quickly, this leader will change his priorities to reflect the time that is being considered in the decisions. Cost reductions, personnel changes and perceived urgency are almost certain outcomes.

These contrasting scenarios are used to show the importance of a leader's time perspective in decision-making. A leader should think about where the finish line really is. Do you borrow from the future to make the present look better? Is what happens this week or month important enough to risk something (or someone) in the future?

Time perspective in leadership is important. It's another thing we need to get right to make good decisions about people and strategy.

The One Thing: _____

_____

Playbook Notes: _____

_____

_____

_____

_____

> "The moment you feel the need to tightly manage someone, you know you've made a hiring mistake. The best people don't need to be managed. Guided, taught and led, yes... but not tightly managed".
>
> **-Jim Collins**

HOW TO HIRE AN EXCEPTIONAL LEADER

HIRING EXCELLENT LEADERS and coaches is crucial for any organization that wants to grow and thrive, and finding capable leadership is not easy. Bad recruiting decisions are costly, and they're very easy to make. Hiring an ineffective leader or manager can be a huge setback for a company or department.

Let's contrast a poor leadership hire with the hiring of an unsuccessful non-leader. When we hire a weak or ineffective salesperson, administrator, staffer, coder, receptionist, floor person, etc., their individual performance typically becomes apparent very quickly. Their lack of results or professionalism will usually be noticed and acted upon with minimal risk to the team.

When we hire an ineffective leader, it usually takes much longer to identify the cause of the poor results. The performance of the ineffective leader will show up first in his team or department's results. Often, a team is initially held responsible for poor leadership. We've all seen situations where it took months or even years to realize that bad results or outcomes were actually a reflection of poor leadership or ineffective coaching.

Why is hiring effective leaders so challenging? Here are a few of the reasons:

» Many experienced leaders and managers are not direct producers, so it's hard to get objective information about their personal performance.

» Interviewers are often influenced by aspects of a candidate that have nothing to do with leadership.

» Hiring companies and recruiters tend to sort candidates by title and experience. We all know that a person can have an impressive title and lots of years of experience on their resume... and still be an ineffective leader.

» Often, a newly-hired leader is replacing an ineffective leader... so the performance bar can be set very low at the start. It can take a while to realize that things aren't improving with the new leader.

The good news is that there's a lot you can do to improve your odds at hiring an exceptional leader. Dynamic, growth-oriented organizations should be as diligent as possible with the recruitment of leaders. Finding the right person for your leadership role will pay off in many important ways. There are proven tactics for taking some of the risk out of hiring leaders. Let's review the top six:

THE TOP SIX TACTICS FOR IDENTIFYING EXCEPTIONAL LEADERS:

1. <u>Ask for 360° references</u>. That's references from superiors, peers and... most importantly... people whom this candidate has led in the past. You will hear a lot about the candidate's personality in these conversations. Make sure you ask about specific coaching skills and priorities, that's what you really want to know. You'll get an excellent understanding of your candidates actual capability from this 360° view.

2. <u>Ask the candidate how she has deployed different leadership skills for different situations</u>. Having "Manager" or "VP" on your business card does not make you a leader, but a leveragable skill-set does. Have them explain how their leadership has evolved through the different management roles on their resume.

3. <u>Ask the candidate about thought leaders who have influenced his leadership</u>. Whose books, blogs, talks and ideas resonate with him? If a leader is not actively looking for inspiration and education, they are not going to evolve and improve over time. They will have a limited positive impact on your organization.

4. <u>Figure out if your candidate has an internal or external motivational drive</u>. We want internally-driven leaders, their performance lid is much higher than their externally-driven peers. Here's a great question to find out: Ask your candidate "how do you know when you are doing a great

job as a leader?" The externally-driven leader will talk about recognition and targets, the internally driven leader will usually talk about progress with their team, organizational culture or the development of their own leadership skills.

5. Ask about a time where they have failed as a leader or coach. Any progressive leader will have a list of disappointments where their results didn't match their expectations. Listen carefully to where they assign blame. Do they own it… or do they pass it off on their people or to uncontrollable circumstances? You want to hire a fully accountable leader.

6. Have a candid conversation with your candidate about leadership. Ask them how they define it, and how they would go about coaching the team and driving growth at your organization. Ask about short and long-term tactics. Listen closely for ideas about organized initiatives, actionable tactics, and coaching strategies. Be wary of the leader who only talks about motivational ideas. Motivational tactics… both positive and negative… are typically overemphasized by underdeveloped leaders.

Do you remember this famous Eleanor Roosevelt quote?

"Great minds discuss ideas; average minds discuss circumstances & events; small minds discuss other people"

It is surprisingly applicable to recruiting and interviewing. The exceptional candidate will show a lot of enthusiasm and passion for leadership and coaching. They will be excited about working with a new team and helping them discover more of their own capability. Average candidates will want to talk about their old bosses, or things that happened to them in previous roles. Ask a lot of open-ended questions to determine your candidate's orientation.

Those are the top six ways to hire an exceptional leader. Remember, finding the right leader is the first step in taking your organization or department to the next level. You want a fully engaged leader with the skills to do amazing things in your organization. Don't be hasty in your decision… it's a big one.

The One Thing: _____

_____

Playbook Notes: _____

_____

_____

_____

> "The objective of leadership is to help those who are doing poorly to do well and to help those who are doing well to do even better."
>
> **– Jim Rohn**

THERE'S ONLY ONE WAY TO MEASURE LEADERSHIP

THERE'S NO SHORTAGE of information on how to be an effective leader. Anyone who is interested in being a successful leader or manager can keep themselves busy researching and studying the attributes of great leaders.

Often, the attributes of successful leaders are presented as character traits. Experts tell us that the best leaders share these qualities and that the best way to evolve as a leader is to focus on developing these leadership traits. The traits most often mentioned are vision, integrity, confidence, intelligence, decisiveness, and accountability. We're also told that the best leaders are excellent communicators and inspirational to their followers.

There's no argument that these are all very positive attributes, but does having some or all of these qualities really make you an effective leader? Maybe, or maybe not. The personal attributes of a leader are important, but they're not a measure of leadership effectiveness. To say it another way, having some of these traits would be a real asset for any leader, but are they are a reliable way to know if a leader is succeeding in their role? No, they are not.

Leadership is a verb, it is something you do. Leadership can't be measured by listing the attributes of the leader, even if those attributes are very positive. There's not a reliable correlation between leadership attributes and leadership results. That's the bad news. The good news is that leadership is 100% quantifiable. It's easy to measure and easy to see if a leader is succeeding in their role. Here's how:

When a leader is successful, the people they are leading improve over time.

Leadership is all about performance, and it, it shows up in the numbers. Your leadership is reflected with absolute, merciless accuracy in the performance of your team. Poor performers should improve over time, medium performers should be trending positively, and top performers should continue to excel and exceed. When we measure a leader or manager in any other way, we risk measuring things that are out of the leaders control.

The bottom line is that exceptional leaders can drive performance improvements using any of the attributes and characteristics listed previously. Those leadership character traits may allow the leader to get results with his or her team, and the results will tell us if the leader is succeeding. The only real way to measure leadership is by measuring the results of the team.

The One Thing: _____

_____

Playbook Notes: _____

_____

_____

_____

> "A leader's real "authority" is a power you voluntarily give him".
>
> **-David Foster Wallace**

THE LAST WORD

SOMETIMES THE CLEAREST view of something comes from a non-expert. Their language and descriptions are usually original and not influenced by other sources. This is especially true when the subject is leadership. Very few topics have been written about and discussed as much as leadership, and a clear, unbiased view from a non-expert can be hard to find. In his 2000 essay Up, Simba: Seven Days on the Trail of an Anticandidate, the celebrated author David Foster Wallace considers leadership:

"The weird thing is that the word "leader" itself is cliché and boring, but when you come across somebody who actually is a real leader, that person isn't clichéd or boring at all; in fact he's the opposite of clichéd and boring.

Obviously, a real leader isn't just somebody who has ideas you agree with, nor is it just somebody you happen to believe is a good person. Think about it. A real leader is somebody who, because of his own particular power and charisma and example, is able to inspire people, with "inspire" being used here in a serious way. A real leader can somehow get us to do certain things that deep down we think are important and want to be able to do... but usually can't get ourselves to do on our own. It's a mysterious quality, and hard to define, but we always know it when we see it, even as kids. You can probably remember seeing it in certain really great coaches, or teachers, or some extremely cool older kid you looked up to and wanted to be just like.

Some of us remember seeing the quality as kids in a minister or rabbi, or a scoutmaster, or a parent, or a friend's parent, or a supervisor in a summer job. And yes, all these are authority figures, but it's a special kind of authority. If you've ever spent time in the military, you know how incredibly easy it is to tell which of your superiors are real leaders and which aren't, and how little rank has to do with it.

A leader's real "authority" is a power you voluntarily give him, and you grant him this authority not with resentment or resignation but happily; it just feels right. Deep down, you almost always like how a real leader makes you feel, the way you find yourself working harder and pushing yourself and thinking in ways you couldn't ever get to on your own.

In other words, a real leader is somebody who can help us overcome the limitations of our own individual laziness and selfishness and weakness and fear and get us to do better things than we can get ourselves to do on our own."

Isn't that a refreshing and inspiring view of leaders? We think so. It's a nice reminder in a time when the qualities of leadership and leaders are not as clear as they could be.

GOING FORWARD

We want to thank you for spending some time with this book. We know that if you're reading the last words, in the last chapter, of a leadership book you are a very special person. The experts tell us that fewer than 20% of people actually finish non-fiction books. Clearly, you are someone who is intent on making a difference with people. You are serious about the positive influence a progressive leader can have on the world. We hope you've already put some of the recommendations and ideas you read here to use.

Our intent with The Exceptional Leaders Playbook is that it is a true working resource for you with actionable strategies you'll add to your working leadership skill set over time.

You're in a privileged position as a leader. You are steering people and organizations to where you think they should go. Sometimes this responsibility means that you will have to learn new things, or new ways to do things. It is your responsibility to craft a vision of the future that everyone can participate in. You must keep working on your leadership skills and expectations, they will set the "lid" for your team's performance potential. We all know that there's absolutely no limit to the positive influence a leader can have with people. Your job is to gradually translate your leadership vision into reality.

The One Thing: _____

_____

Playbook Notes: _____

_____

_____

_____

_____

> "If you're not willing to learn, no one can help you. If you're determined to learn, no one can stop you."
>
> **-Earl Nightingale**

LET'S STAY CONNECTED!

THE EXCEPTIONAL LEADERS LAB is an international leadership organization focused on developing leaders at all levels. We provide innovative programs and progressive strategies designed to help organizations and individuals reach their ultimate potential.

After registering on our website **ExceptionalLeadersLab. com**, you will receive fresh, free, leadership and self-development content delivered weekly along with access to additional progressive development resources like other books, videos, webinars and workshops. Of course, we will keep your contact information private.

Please connect with us on LinkedIn, Facebook and Twitter for fresh ideas and resources for your personal and professional development.

Remember, leadership is a verb. It is something you DO. We hope you have leveraged some of what you read here already, and encourage you to revisit sections when you need a fresh approach.

Your partners in leadership,

Tracy Spears & Wally Schmader

Founder & CEO

Exceptional Leaders Lab

> "Feeling gratitude and not expressing it is like wrapping a present and not giving it."
>
> **-William Arthur Ward**

THE "THANK YOU" PAGE

IT'S DAUNTING TO EVEN ATTEMPT to thank everyone who has supported us in our journey to grow a world class leadership training company. The following list is by no means a complete list of the people that we are grateful to:

Rosemary Harris	Ronda Baucom
Bonnie Foxworth	Elizabeth Stewart
Justin Sachs	Jim Stovall
Ana Maddox	Jason Maddox
Robert Babcock	Lisa Beard
Michael Brothers	Chase Delozier
ELL Lab Partners	Tom & Michelle Morris
Carol Seymour	Jane Wiseman

If you have ever read one of our blogs, hired us to come to your company, referred us to a colleague, purchased a webinar or online course, asked us to deliver a keynote or break out session, purchased a book, liked a comment on Facebook, retweeted a tweet, clicked on the heart on Instagram, connected with us on Linkedin, or supported our efforts in any way....please know we are grateful.

NOTES:

Notes:

CPSIA information can be obtained
at www.ICGtesting.com
Printed in the USA
LVOW13*2158140318
569925LV00003B/3/P

9 781628 654639